Conquering Fifth Grade

Reading
Mathematics
Science
Social Studies
Writing

Jennifer Prior, Ph.D.

Publishing Credits

Corinne Burton, M.A.Ed., *President*; Conni Medina, M.A.Ed., *Managing Editor*; Emily R. Smith, M.A.Ed., *Content Director*; Lynette Ordoñez, *Editor*; Evan Ferrell, *Graphic Designer*; Lubabah Memon, *Assistant Editor*

Image Credits

All images from iStock and Shutterstock.

Standards

Shell Education
A division of Teacher Created Materials
5301 Oceanus Drive
Huntington Beach, CA 92649-1030

www.tcmpub.com/shell-education
ISBN 978-1-4258-1624-7

Printed by 977
Printed in USA PO# PO16780

Table of Contents

Dear Family,

Welcome to *Conquering Fifth Grade*. Fifth grade will be an exciting and challenging year for your child. This book is designed to supplement the concepts your child is learning in fifth grade and to strengthen the connection between home and school. The activities in this book are based on today's standards and provide practice in reading, word study, language, writing, mathematics, social studies, and science. It also features fun, yet challenging, critical-thinking activities and games. In addition to the activity sheets in this book, the end of each section also provides engaging extension activities.

Your child should complete one unit per month, including the extension activities. This will allow your child to think about grade-level concepts over a longer period of time. This also ensures that the book can be completed in one school year.

Keep these tips in mind as you work with your child this year:

- Set aside specific times each week to work on the activities.
- Have your child complete one or two activities each time, rather than an entire unit at one time.
- Keep all practice sessions with your child positive and constructive. If the mood becomes tense or you and your child get frustrated, set the book aside and find another time to practice.
- Help your child with instructions, if necessary. If your child is having difficulty understanding what to do, work through some of the problems together.
- Encourage your child to do his or her best work, and compliment the effort that goes into learning.

Enjoy the time learning with your child during fifth grade. Summer will be here before you know it!

Sincerely,

The Shell Education Staff

Suggested Family Activities

You can extend your child's learning by taking fun family field trips. A wide variety of experiences helps expand and develop a child's vocabulary. Field trips also provide greater context and meaning to his or her learning in school.

A Trip to a Zoo

Bring a blank world map on a clipboard with you. As you visit each animal, have your child read the information placard and determine the original location of the animal or species. Then, have your child write the name of the animal on its location on the map. You'll be amazed by how diverse the animals in your local zoo really are!

A Trip to a Museum

Your first stop should be the gift shop. Have your child pick out five postcards of artifacts or paintings in the museum. Then, as you visit the museum, your child should be on the lookout for the five items he or she chose. It's an individual scavenger hunt! If your child finds all five, you can celebrate the accomplishment! Plus, your child gets to keep the postcards as mementos of the day.

A Trip to a Library

Work with your child to find a paired fiction and nonfiction set to read. First, think of a topic your child likes to learn about. Your child can then use the digital catalog to search for books on this topic that match his or her reading level. Your child can choose one fiction book and one nonfiction book on the same topic, check them out, and enjoy expanding his or her mind!

A Trip to a Monument or Memorial

Ahead of time, look up some interesting stories about the person who is honored by the monument/memorial. Focus on stories about the person's childhood or early accomplishments, as those will be more relatable to your child. As you stand and look at the monument/memorial, tell the stories and ask your child what kind of monument/memorial could be built for him or her someday!

A Trip to a National Park

The National Park Service has a great program called Junior Rangers. If you go to a local park, check in with the rangers at the visitors center to see what tasks your child can complete to earn a Junior Ranger patch and/or certificate. Your child can also go to the WebRangers site (www.nps.gov/webrangers) and check out a vacation spot, play games, and earn virtual rewards!

Suggested Family Activities *(cont.)*

By discussing the activities in this book, you can enhance your child's learning. But it doesn't have to stop there. The suggestions below provide even more ideas on how to support your child's education.

General Skills

- Make sure your child gets plenty of exercise. Children need about 60 minutes of physical activity each day. You may want to have your child sign up for a sport. Or you can do fun things as a family, such as swimming, riding bicycles, or hiking.
- Help your child become organized and responsible. Have places for your child to keep important things. Take time to set up a schedule together. Use a timer to keep track of time spent on different activities.

Reading Skills

- Set a reading time for the entire family at least once every other day. You can read aloud or read silently. Help your child choose books that are at comfortable reading levels and are interesting to him or her.
- After reading, talk to your child about what he or she has read. Encourage your child to share details.
- Read books to your child that are above his or her reading level. This allows him or her to experience more complex vocabulary, sentences, and ideas.

Writing Skills

- Encourage your child to write emails, texts, or letters to friends and family members who live near and far.
- Have your child create an online blog or keep a diary/journal about activities he or she is doing during time off from school.

Mathematics Skills

- Have your child estimate measurements while out in the community. For example: *This menu is about 8 inches wide. About how wide do you think the table is?*
- Involve your child in cooking dinner. This is a great way to teach about fractions, as well as liquid and dry units of measure.

Directions: Read the text, and answer the questions.

I Want a Puppy

Nick wanted a puppy, so he decided to become a volunteer at the animal shelter. He was hoping to convince his parents that he was ready to take care of a puppy. He volunteered at the shelter twice each week—on Tuesdays after school and on Saturdays.

Nick did several things to volunteer. He walked the dogs, he washed them, and he brushed them. Grooming the long-haired dogs took a long time! He cleaned the dogs' kennels, too. He also played with the puppies to get them used to people. Occasionally, Nick spent time with the kittens and cats, but he preferred working with the dogs. There was always plenty to do at the shelter, so Nick was never bored.

1. What does the first sentence tell about this text?
   - (A) This text is about volunteering at an animal shelter.
   - (B) This text is about taking shelter during a storm.
   - (C) This text is about adopting an animal.
   - (D) This text is about different animals.

2. To which word can the suffix *–ing* be added?
   - (A) also
   - (B) dogs
   - (C) care
   - (D) plenty

3. What is a *kennel*?
   - (A) a place for animals
   - (B) a kind of food
   - (C) a piece of clothing
   - (D) a helper

4. What does *occasionally* mean?
   - (A) often
   - (B) never
   - (C) once in a while
   - (D) daily

Directions: Read the text, and answer the questions.

Government Branches

The U.S. government has three branches. One branch is the executive branch. That branch is in charge of running the government. The president of the United States is the head of the executive branch. Another branch is the legislative branch. That branch is in charge of making laws. It also controls taxes, prints money, and does other important jobs. Congress heads the legislative branch. The third branch of government is the judicial branch. That branch is in charge of making sure that laws are fair. It interprets the most important set of laws, the Constitution. The judicial branch is also in charge of making sure that anyone accused of a crime gets a fair trial. The Supreme Court is the head of the judicial branch.

1. Which word best summarizes what the text is about?
   - (A) president
   - (B) accused
   - (C) government
   - (D) trial

2. Which branch of government is in charge of making sure laws are fair?
   - (A) the president of the United States
   - (B) the executive branch
   - (C) the legislative branch
   - (D) the judicial branch

3. Why is *Constitution* capitalized?
   - (A) It is the last word in a sentence.
   - (B) It is the first word in a sentence.
   - (C) *Constitution* is a proper noun.
   - (D) The president is the head of the executive branch.

4. What is the meaning of the word *head* in this text?
   - (A) the leader
   - (B) the mind
   - (C) the start of something
   - (D) a part of the body

Directions: The words in the Word Bank all end in the suffix *–ant*. Look up any words you don't know. Then, use each word in a sentence.

Word Bank

- defendant
- immigrant
- assistant
- brilliant
- ignorant
- compliant
- irritant
- extravagant
- vibrant
- observant

1. ______________________________
2. ______________________________
3. ______________________________
4. ______________________________
5. ______________________________
6. ______________________________
7. ______________________________
8. ______________________________
9. ______________________________
10. ______________________________

Directions: Write the missing punctuation in each sentence.

1. If Ben Franklin had gotten his way the turkey would be the national bird

2. When you get on a plane you might not worry about other flying things

3. For thousands of years people have been lifting weights

4. Charles Lindbergh a pilot was famous for his flying

5. I can't believe that you my best friend said that

6. On April 22 1970 the first Earth Day was held

7. Many writers such as Scott O'Dell may take nearly a year to write a book

8. Leo Lionni was born in Amsterdam Holland

9. When the United States had its 100th birthday it got a big present

10. Did you know that J K Rowling helps children in need

Directions: Place check marks in the circles with sentences that could be included in an informative/explanatory paragraph about the blue-ringed octopus.

I don't like them.

The small octopus shouted, "I will get you!"

They are found in Japan and Australia.

Their skin is gray, yellow, or tan with light blue rings.

They use a powerful poison to paralyze their prey.

They are about the size of golf balls.

When they are threatened, the rings on their skin turn bright blue.

You need to help save these tiny creatures.

Directions: Write an informative/explanatory paragraph about the blue-ringed octopus. Use the facts from page 11 to help you.

Remember!

A strong informative/explanatory paragraph:

- stays on topic
- does not include personal opinions
- includes facts, details, and definitions

Directions: Solve each problem.

1. $\begin{array}{r} 30 \\ \times \quad 4 \\ \hline \end{array}$

2. $\begin{array}{r} 57 \\ \times \quad 8 \\ \hline \end{array}$

3. $\begin{array}{r} 126 \\ \times \quad 71 \\ \hline \end{array}$

4. $\begin{array}{r} 77 \\ \times \quad 28 \\ \hline \end{array}$

5. $\begin{array}{r} 209 \\ \times \quad 30 \\ \hline \end{array}$

6. $\begin{array}{r} 448 \\ \times \quad 16 \\ \hline \end{array}$

7. $\begin{array}{r} 87 \\ \times \quad 8 \\ \hline \end{array}$

8. $\begin{array}{r} 352 \\ \times \quad 9 \\ \hline \end{array}$

9. $\begin{array}{r} 256 \\ \times \quad 5 \\ \hline \end{array}$

10. $\begin{array}{r} 322 \\ \times \quad 13 \\ \hline \end{array}$

UNIT 1

Mathematics

Directions: Solve each problem.

1. $2\overline{)564}$

2. $9\overline{)144}$

3. $18\overline{)486}$

4. $6\overline{)514}$

5. $12\overline{)498}$

6. $14\overline{)112}$

7. $5\overline{)277}$

8. $22\overline{)704}$

Directions: Read the problem, and answer the questions.

A bookstore orders 175 dozen pencils. How many pencils are there in all?

1. What information is given?

____

____

2. What strategy can you use to solve the problem?

____

____

____

3. Can you think of a different way to show the problem? Explain your thinking.

____

____

____

4. Solve the problem.

____

Directions: Read and solve each problem.

Problem 1: A bookstore orders 162 dozen pencils. How many pencils are there in all?

List What You Know	State Your Plan
Solve the Problem	**Look Back and Explain**

Problem 2: The bookstore also orders 36 packages of erasers. The erasers come in packs of 25. How many erasers are there in all?

List What You Know	State Your Plan
Solve the Problem	**Look Back and Explain**

Directions: An entrepreneur is a person who designs, launches, and runs a business. This kind of person takes a lot of risk because the business may or may not be successful. Imagine that you are an entrepreneur, and answer the questions.

1. Think about a way you could become an entrepreneur. What kind of product or service could you sell?

 ____

 ____

2. What problem might be solved by your product or service?

 ____

 ____

3. Draw a picture showing your invention or how people would use your service.

4. Who would most likely be interested in this product or service (the general population, children, moms, business people, chefs, etc.)?

 ____

 ____

5. How much would you charge for the product or service?

 ____

Directions: Follow the steps in this experiment to find out what is magnetic.

What You Need

- two bar magnets
- small objects

What to Do

1. Hold small objects near one of the magnets to see if the objects are attracted to it. List your results in the chart.

Attracted to the Magnet	Not Attracted to the Magnet

2. How can you move one magnet without touching it? Try your idea, and describe how well it works.

____

____

3. Hold one magnet up to another. What happens?

____

4. Reverse the magnet. What happens now?

____

Directions: Every mini-grid must have each of the numbers 1–6. Every column must have each of the numbers 1–6. Every row must have each of the numbers 1–6.

5				4	
4			6		5
	6			1	
		1	2		
1			5		4
	5	4		2	

Directions: Play with a partner. Roll two number cubes. Use the chart to match your roll to an object and a price. Then, roll a second time. Add the cost of your two items. Have your partner roll twice and add the cost of his or her items. The player with the least expensive purchase wins! Continue until both players have had 10 turns.

Roll	Item	Price
2		$5.47
3	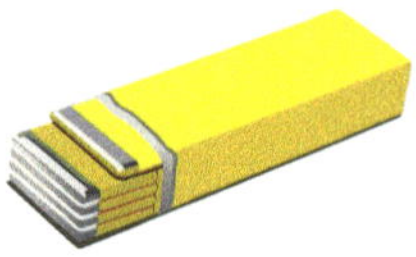	$0.54
4		$2.98
5		$8.66
6		$15.32

Roll	Item	Price
7		$10.86
8		$0.34
9		$16.57
10		$2.43
11		$0.65
12		$18.79

Spelling Activity

Look up the meaning of the suffix *–ant*. Explain how the suffix affects the meaning of each spelling word from page 9.

Writing Activity

Review your paragraph on page 12. Check your writing for proper punctuation.

Mathematics Activity

Choose one of the problems from pages 13–14, and write a word problem for it. How do you know that your word problem can be solved the same way?

Social Studies Activity

Share your product or service idea with a family member. Discuss what it would actually take to get the project off the ground as a real business.

Science Activity

What did the things attracted to the magnet have in common? Form a hypothesis about what is attracted to magnets.

Listening-and-Speaking Activity

Tell your family or friends about what entrepreneurs do, and explain how being an entrepreneur can be risky.

Directions: Read the text, and answer the questions.

Linda's Glasses

Mrs. Curtis said, "Make sure you write this assignment down, everyone. It's important."

"Mrs. Curtis," Linda said. "I can't see the assignment."

Mrs. Curtis suggested, "Come up to the front of the room to copy it."

Linda moved to the front of the room, copied the assignment into her notebook, and returned to her seat. When class was over, Mrs. Curtis asked Linda to remain. "I'm concerned, Linda, because it seems you're having trouble seeing the board. The school nurse will be checking everyone's vision tomorrow. You should probably tell her about it," Mrs. Curtis said.

"Do you think I'll need glasses?" Linda asked in a concerned voice.

"Maybe," Mrs. Curtis admitted. "But if you do, you'll be able to pick out your very own pair at the optometrist's office. Then, you'll be able to see much more clearly."

"Oh, that sounds fantastic!" Linda said with relief.

1. Which alternative title would best fit this text?
   - (A) "School Day"
   - (B) "A Problem in Class"
   - (C) "Assignment Time"
   - (D) "Mrs. Curtis's Day"

2. Which is a synonym for *assignment*?
   - (A) task
   - (B) board
   - (C) notebook
   - (D) paper

3. What does *remain* mean in this text?
   - (A) to leave
   - (B) to stay behind
   - (C) to be left over
   - (D) to be important

4. Which word describes Mrs. Curtis and her feelings?
   - (A) important
   - (B) angry
   - (C) unsympathetic
   - (D) concerned

Directions: Read the text, and answer the questions.

Breakfast Options

There are many healthy choices for breakfast. One good choice is eggs. Eggs have a lot of protein, and protein helps your body grow. Protein is also important for making your muscles strong. Protein helps stop hunger, too, so you feel more satisfied when you eat. Some people prefer fresh fruit for breakfast. Fresh fruit is very nutritious, too. For example, a banana and yogurt make a tasty and healthy breakfast; so does a fruit smoothie. Experts recommend that people avoid high-fat breakfast foods, such as doughnuts. They are not healthy options, and they do not really satisfy your hunger. It is wiser to choose a breakfast that has whole grains, fruit, and protein. What will you have for breakfast tomorrow?

1. Which prediction is most accurate after previewing the first sentence of the text?
   - Ⓐ The text is about health class.
   - Ⓑ The text is about diets.
   - Ⓒ The text is about eating healthy food.
   - Ⓓ The text is about skipping breakfast.

2. Which word has the same vowel sound as *feel*?
   - Ⓐ red
   - Ⓑ wet
   - Ⓒ hear
   - Ⓓ knew

3. Which means the opposite of *wiser*?
   - Ⓐ smaller
   - Ⓑ more foolish
   - Ⓒ better
   - Ⓓ smarter

4. What does it mean if something *satisfies your hunger*?
   - Ⓐ It takes a long time to eat.
   - Ⓑ It tastes delicious.
   - Ⓒ It makes you even hungrier.
   - Ⓓ It stops your hunger.

Directions: All of the words below end in the suffix *–able*. Write the root word on the first line. Then, write the whole word on the second line.

1. desirable

   ____________________ ____________________

2. excitable

   ____________________ ____________________

3. breakable

   ____________________ ____________________

4. adaptable

   ____________________ ____________________

5. allowable

   ____________________ ____________________

6. comfortable

   ____________________ ____________________

7. distinguishable

   ____________________ ____________________

8. inhabitable

   ____________________ ____________________

9. adorable

   ____________________ ____________________

10. believable

   ____________________ ____________________

Directions: Circle any words that should be capitalized.

1. Soldiers in ancient china had to pass lifting tests.

2. He grew up in Atlanta, georgia.

3. There had been a massive oil spill in santa Barbara, California.

4. In many cities, such as chicago, you can help by being a foster caregiver.

5. That year, william Blackstone gave a birthday present to his wife.

6. Funk-style dancing developed in california at about the same time.

7. try to do sixty minutes of exercise three times a week.

8. Most mosquito bites are just annoying, but some spread the West nile virus.

9. sara and kenny spend a lot of time building forts together.

10. why do people always think i like to swim in the ocean?

Directions: Read the facts about Scotland's Loch Ness Monster. How do you feel about people spending time and money looking for the monster? Complete the graphic organizer.

Loch Ness Monster

- Loch Ness is a body of freshwater in Scotland.
- Loch Ness is about 800 feet (244 meters) deep and 23 miles (37 kilometers) wide.
- The Loch Ness Monster is often called Nessie.
- There are reported sightings of the monster from nearly 1,500 years ago.
- Recent expeditions have used sonar technology to try and find the Loch Ness Monster.
- A famous picture of the Loch Ness Monster from 1933 was recently proven to be a fake.
- Modern underwater photographs show what appears to be a giant flipper.

My Opinion

____

____

My Reasons

1. ______________________________
2. ______________________________
3. ______________________________

My Strong Conclusion

____

____

Directions: Some people believe in the Loch Ness Monster, and some people don't. Draft an opinion paragraph describing how you feel about people continuing to spend time and money looking for the monster. Use the graphic organizer on page 26 to help you.

Remember!

A strong opinion paragraph should include:

- a clearly stated opinion
- reasons that support your opinion
- a strong concluding sentence that restates your opinion

Directions: Solve each problem. Give all answers in simplest terms.

1. Write 0.45 as a fraction.

____

2. Write the decimal for the shaded part on the hundred grid.

____

3. Write $\frac{75}{100}$ as a decimal.

____

4. What is $\frac{1}{3}$ of 12?

____

5. Is $\frac{2}{5}$ equal to $\frac{4}{10}$?

____

6. Write 0.25 as a fraction.

____

7. Is $\frac{1}{2}$ greater than, less than, or equal to $\frac{1}{5}$?

____

8. What is $\frac{1}{6}$ of 4?

____

9. What is $\frac{1}{8}$ of 24?

____

10. Write $\frac{66}{100}$ as a decimal.

____

11. Shade the grid to show $\frac{51}{100}$.

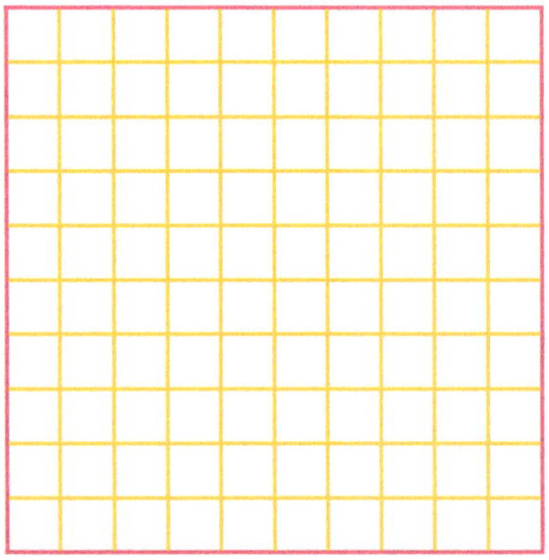

12. Write 0.94 as a fraction.

____

Directions: Solve each problem.

1. $15 + 5 = 20 - \square$
2. $10 \times \square = 5 \times 8$
3. $56 + 10 = 75 - \square$
4. $7 \times 5 = 40 - \square$
5. $70 - 35 = 20 + \square$
6. $46 + \square = 45 + 8$
7. $20 \times 2 = 5 \times \square$
8. $65 - \square = 3 \times 20$
9. $36 + \square = 27 + 22$
10. $78 + 6 = 92 - \square$
11. $8 \times 3 = \square \times 12$
12. $68 - \square = 8 \times 8$

Directions: Think about the problem, and answer the questions.

Problem 1: Central Middle School needs to put students into groups of 14 for their upcoming field days. There are 1,572 students at the school. How many groups will there be? Will there be any students left over?

List What You Know	State Your Plan
Solve the Problem	**Look Back and Explain**

Problem 2: North Middle School is putting their students in groups of 8 for their upcoming field days. There are 936 students at the school. How many groups will there be? Will there be any students left over?

List What You Know	State Your Plan
Solve the Problem	**Look Back and Explain**

Directions: Show two ways to solve the problem.

1. Maya needs to distribute 7,632 packages of paper to 36 classrooms. How many packages of paper will each classroom receive?

Strategy 1

Strategy 2

2. Which strategy do you like better? Explain your reasoning.

____

____

____

____

Directions: Look at Jose's current budget on the left. How could he revise his budget to save for a vacation? Use the guidelines in the box to create a revised budget for Jose. Then, answer the questions.

- Jose cannot spend more than $2,200 per month.
- The budgets for food, utilities, rent, and car payment cannot be lowered.
- Jose can spend less or nothing at all on things that are not essential.

Current Budget		Revised Budget	
Food	$300	Food	
Utilities (electricity/water)	$100	Utilities (electricity/water)	
Rent	$1,000	Rent	
Car payment	$350	Car payment	
Cable TV and Internet	$150	Cable TV and Internet	
Cell phone	$100	Cell phone	
Entertainment (movies, eating out)	$100	Entertainment (movies, eating out)	
Savings and Emergency Fund	$100	Savings and Emergency Fund	
Vacation savings	$0	Vacation savings	
Total	**$2,200**	**Total**	

What changes did you make and why?

____

____

____

Directions: Follow the steps in this experiment to find out what *positive* and *negative* mean.

What You Need

- two C batteries
- electrical wire
- electrical tape
- LED (Light Emitting Diode)

What to Do

1. Look at your batteries. Find the ends marked with the + symbol. Find the ends marked with the – symbol.

2. Tape the two C batteries side by side so that one + end is next to a – end.

3. Look at your LED. You will find one of two things. Some LEDs have two leads of different lengths. The long lead is the + lead. The short lead is the – lead. Other LEDs will have thick and thin leads of the same length. The thin lead is the + lead. The thick lead is the – lead.

4. Use electrical tape to connect the + and – ends of the battery to the + and – leads of the LED. Does it matter which end of the battery is connected to which lead of the LED? Why?

   ____

   ____

5. Why do you think batteries and electrical devices have + and – parts?

   ____

   ____

   ____

UNIT 2

Critical Thinking

Directions: Some common items can have different uses. For example, an ice cube tray could be used to hold nails and screws. Describe an alternative use for each item.

1. serving spoon

____

2. hammer

____

3. hairbrush

____

4. hanger

____

5. ironing board

____

6. bookcase

____

7. water bucket

____

8. empty cereal box

____

9. empty soda cans

____

Directions: Play with a partner. Use small objects to mark your places. Roll a number cube. Move that number of spaces. If the space has a word on it, add *–able* to that word, and spell it. If you land on a blank space, think of another word that ends in *–able,* and spell it. The first player to reach the finish wins.

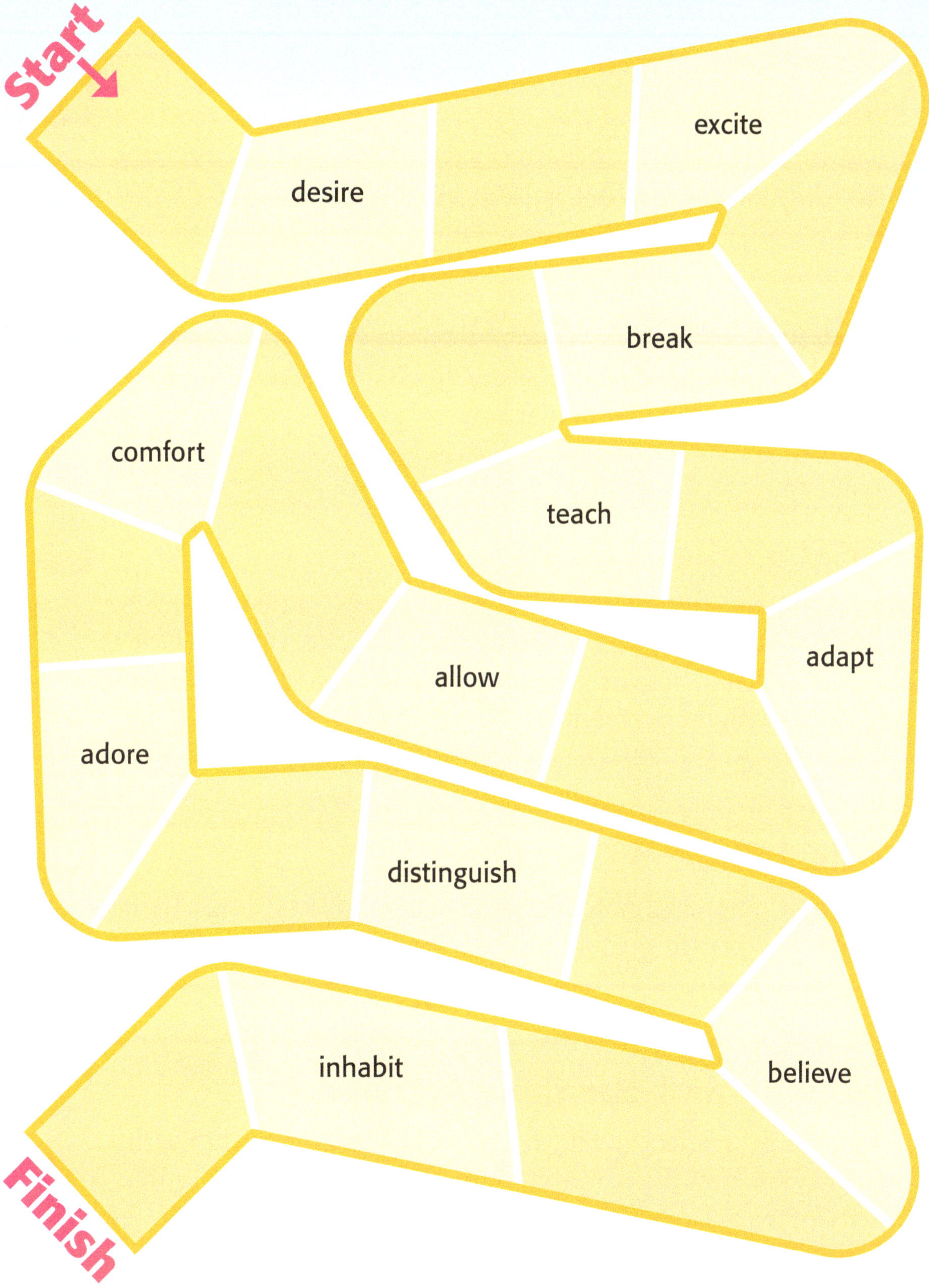

Spelling Activity

Think of three more words that have the suffix *–able*. Use each new word in a sentence.

Writing Activity

Conduct some research to learn three more facts about the Loch Ness Monster. Revise your writing, adding the facts you found.

Problem-Solving Activity

Review the word problems on pages 30–31. Write a word problem that could be solved in a similar way.

Social Studies Activity

Review the social studies activity from page 32. Jose has decided to get a roommate to save more money. Now, he will only have to pay half the rent. Create a new budget showing what you think he should do with the additional $500.

Critical-Thinking Activity

Find three other common items that can be used for other things. Explain how else they could be used to a family member.

Listening-and-Speaking Activity

Ask a family member to tell you his or her first experience with managing money. Listen carefully, and then ask three questions to clarify or expand upon what was said.

Directions: Read the text, and answer the questions.

Furniture Measurements

Douglass and his father were getting ready to buy new furniture and other things that Douglass would need for his room. The first thing they needed to do was measure Douglass's room. His dad retrieved a tape measure and told Douglass, "I'll measure the walls and the floor space, and you write down what I say, okay?" Douglass agreed, and the two excitedly began measuring. Douglass's dad called out the length of each wall, and Douglass recorded the numbers.

When they were finished, Douglass had a list of all of the measurements. Douglass's dad looked at the list and said, "This looks great, Douglass. Now, let's start thinking about what sort of furniture you'll want. You'll need a bed, a desk, and a good, strong chair, so we'll start with those." Douglass couldn't wait to see what his room would look like when it was finished.

1. What does Douglass's dad use to measure the walls and floor space?
   - (A) furniture
   - (B) tape measure
   - (C) desk
   - (D) project

2. What does it mean to *measure* an object?
   - (A) find out the size
   - (B) paint
   - (C) buy furniture
   - (D) write down sizes

3. Which is not an example of *furniture*?
   - (A) a desk
   - (B) a bed
   - (C) a chair
   - (D) a wall

4. Why are they measuring Douglass's room?
   - (A) Douglass will move his things to another room.
   - (B) They are going to move to a new house.
   - (C) They are going to buy new furniture for Douglass.
   - (D) They are going to add a room to the house.

Directions: Read the text, and answer the questions.

Hearing Tests

Have you ever had your hearing tested? Hearing tests let your doctor and your parents know if you have difficulty hearing. Here is how a hearing test works: The school nurse or a doctor has you wear a special set of headphones. Then, you should hear a series of various tones, or sounds. The nurse or doctor directs you to raise your hand or press a button whenever you hear a sound. Some of the sounds are very soft, while others are louder. That helps determine the decibel levels you can hear. Some of the tones are low-pitched, and others are high-pitched. That helps determine the frequencies you can hear. If you cannot hear certain sounds, the test will show that you are having difficulty hearing. Then you, your parents, and your doctor can decide what to do for your hearing.

1. Which picture would tell a reader more about this text?
   - (A) a picture of an ear
   - (B) a picture of a musical note
   - (C) a picture of a person taking a hearing test
   - (D) a picture of a raised hand

2. What is the main idea?
   - (A) Hearing tests tell you if you have trouble hearing.
   - (B) You hear a series of tones.
   - (C) Some sounds are low-pitched.
   - (D) People wear a special set of headphones.

3. Using context clues, which word is the measurement of volume?
   - (A) frequencies
   - (B) decibel
   - (C) headphones
   - (D) tones

4. Which word refers to low-pitched or high-pitched tones?
   - (A) decibels
   - (B) headphones
   - (C) buttons
   - (D) frequencies

Directions: Write each spelling word in print and in cursive.

1. absent

2. surprise

3. function

4. impatient

5. specific

6. consent

7. diligent

8. decadent

9. dilemma

10. leisure

Directions: Read and answer each question.

1. Circle the adverb in the sentence.

   That machine worked well, and other people wanted one.

2. Circle the adjectives in the sentence.

   The huge palace was built about 3,500 years ago.

3. Circle the adverb in the sentence.

   Chimps sometimes use stones as hammers.

4. Circle the adjective in the sentence.

   Heavy backpacks may cause pain.

5. Circle the adjective in the sentence.

   Eskimos call watery snow *mangokpok*.

6. Circle the adverb in the sentence.

   A heavy rainstorm can quickly cause a flash flood.

7. Circle the adverb in the sentence.

   People often get flu shots.

8. Circle the adjectives in the sentence.

   Time flies when we are happy or excited.

Directions: Imagine you are skydiving. You have just jumped out of a plane and are soaring high in the sky. Complete the graphic organizer below by recording specific observations for each of your five senses.

Senses	Detailed Description
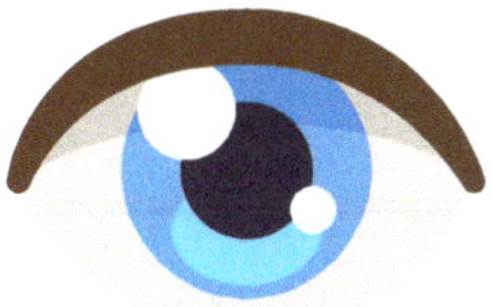	I see…
	I hear…
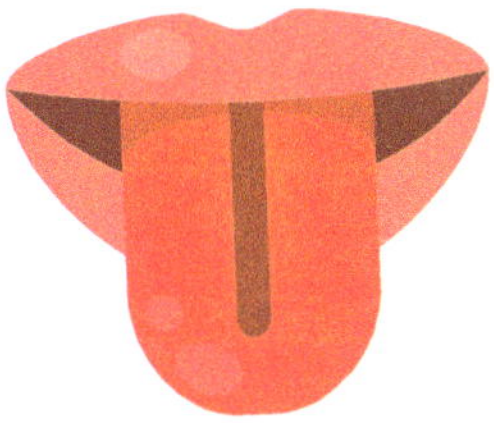	I taste…
	I smell…
	I feel…

Directions: Imagine you are skydiving for the first time. Describe your skydiving experience. Include details about where you dove, who was with you, and how you felt as you stepped out of the plane. Use the graphic organizer on page 41 to help you.

Remember!

You want the reader to imagine that he or she is right there with you jumping out of that plane. Include lots of strong sensory details to paint a vivid picture with your words.

Directions: Solve each problem.

1 **Favorite Foods**

Tacos	Spaghetti	Pizza	Hot Dogs
17	18	26	11

How many more students favor the most popular two foods than the least popular two foods?

____

2 Gary has 23 quarters and 15 dimes in his bank. He saves 4 more quarters each week. He saves 5 more dimes each week. Complete the chart to determine how many dimes he will have at the end of 4 weeks.

	Start	Week 1	Week 2	Week 3	Week 4
quarters	23	27	31	35	39
dimes					

3 What fraction of the people represented in the circle graph favor strawberry?

Favorite Ice Cream

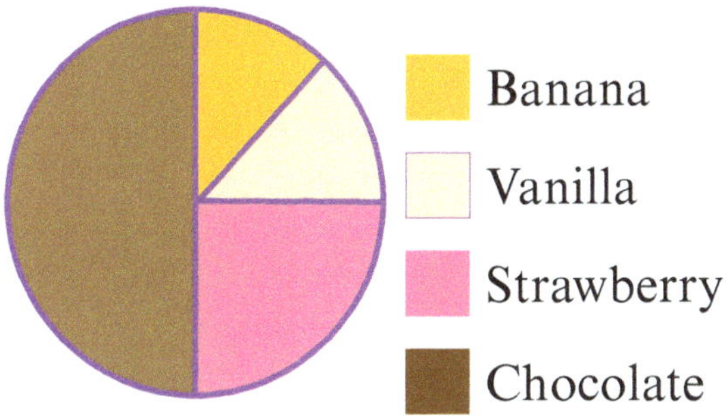

____

4 **Books Read**

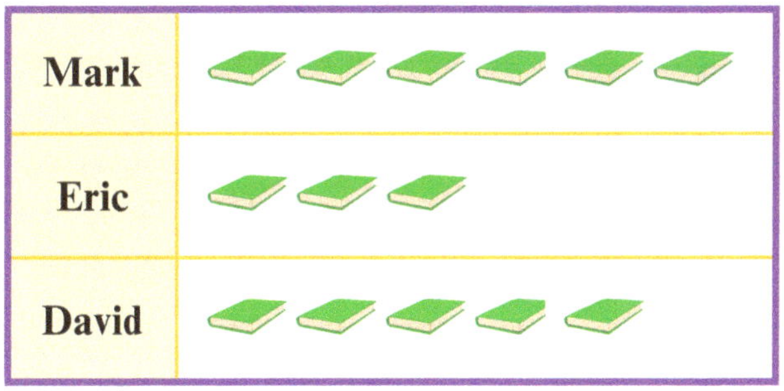

 = 10 books

How many more books did Mark read than Eric?

____

Directions: Solve each problem.

1. Which sports clubs have an equal number of members?

____

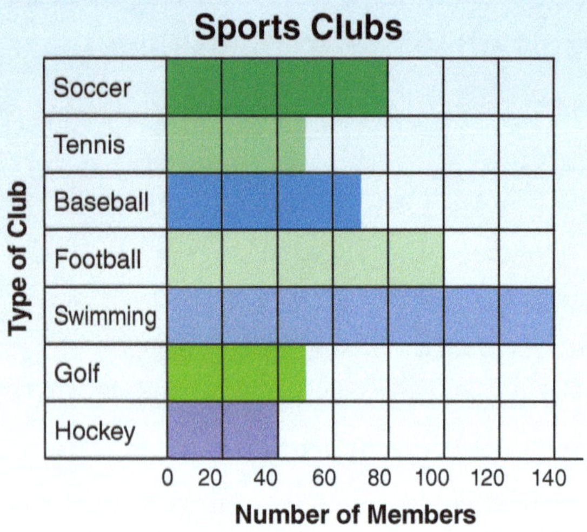

2. What is the total number of books read this year?

____

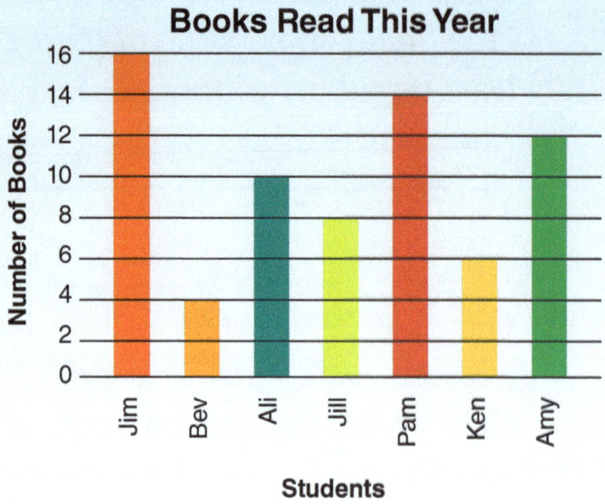

3.

Fish Caught

Juan	Maggi	Max	Erik	Aliki	Tia	Jarome
8	4	5	7	11	4	7

Juan caught two times as many fish as Maggi. Aliki caught _______________ times as many fish as Tia.

4.

Money in Tommy's Bank

Quarters	𝍸 IIII
Dimes	𝍸 𝍸 𝍸 III
Nickels	𝍸 IIII

What is the total value of the money in Tommy's bank?

____

Directions: Read and solve each problem.

Problem 1: Jamila has a gift box that is 8 cm long, 8 cm wide, and 2 cm high. It has a volume of 128 cubic centimeters. She has a second gift box that is the same width but is twice the length and three times the height. What is the volume of the second gift box?

List What You Know	State Your Plan
Solve the Problem	**Look Back and Explain**

Problem 2: Tonya has a tool chest that is 5 feet long, 3 feet wide, and 4 feet high. It has a volume of 60 cubic feet. She has a second tool chest that has the same width, twice the length, and half the height. What is the volume of the second tool chest?

List What You Know	State Your Plan
Solve the Problem	**Look Back and Explain**

Directions: Show two ways to solve the problem.

1. Mrs. Clark is sending a care package to her daughter who is away at college. She needs a box that holds 36 cubic inches. Sketch two different boxes that Mrs. Clark can use to send her package. Write an equation for each sketch to justify your reasoning.

Strategy 1

Strategy 2

2. Do you think there are more than two solutions to this problem? Why or why not?

____

____

____

____

____

Directions: Read the text, and answer the questions.

Bartering

Some people barter for goods and services. Bartering is the practice of paying for goods and services without money. Instead, people pay with other goods and services. For example, if Philip has chickens, he could give eggs to his neighbor in exchange for apples from her tree. Or he could exchange eggs for someone to come mow his lawn. This system has been used for centuries. Most countries today use money instead of bartering. However, friends and family members often barter goods and services informally.

1. How might you barter with your friends and family?

____

____

____

2. What goods and services could you barter?

____

____

____

3. What goods and services would you want to receive in return?

____

____

____

Directions: Follow the steps in this experiment to see how a compass works.

What You Need

- copper wire
- battery
- cardboard tube
- tape
- plastic dish
- tub of water

What to Do

1. Wind about 20 turns of copper wire into a coil around the cardboard tube. Peel the plastic coating off of the ends of the wire.
2. Place the coil in the plastic dish beside the battery. Attach the bare ends of the wires to the battery with tape.
3. Float the plastic dish in the tub of water. What direction does the coil point?
4. Turn the dish to point another way. What happens?

___

___

___

5. This is similar to how a compass works. How is this experiment similar to and different from a hiking compass?

___

___

___

Directions: Read the clues below. Draw the people in order from tallest to shortest. Label each person with his or her height.

- Eliot is 6 inches taller than June.
- June is one foot shorter than Demir.
- At $6\frac{1}{2}$ feet, Demir is the tallest.
- Iris is the shortest.
- Candace is 6 inches shorter than June and 6 inches taller than Iris.

__________ __________ __________ __________ __________

Directions: Play with a partner. Use small objects to mark your places. Take turns rolling one number cube. Move the number of spaces that you roll. Set a timer for 30 seconds. Name three things that could be used for bartering. If the time runs out before you can name three things, move back one space. The first player to reach the finish wins.

Spelling Activity

Find the words on page 39 that end with the suffix *–ent*. Look up the definitions of these words. Explain how the suffix affects their meanings.

Writing Activity

Review your narrative on page 42. Circle the adjectives and adverbs you used to describe the experience of skydiving. Select three words that you circled. Use a thesaurus to find more interesting or vivid words to add to your narrative or to replace your words.

Mathematics Activity

Take a quick survey of your family members. Ask them what type of music or food they like best, or use a different category. Graph your results.

Problem-Solving Activity

Find a rectangular prism in your house. Calculate its volume in cubic centimeters.

Science Activity

Review your experiment from page 48. What do you think would happen if you floated two dishes in the same tub of water? Why?

Listening-and-Speaking Activity

Tell a family member the three most valuable things you learned from Unit 3.

Directions: Read the text, and answer the questions.

The Assignment

Ryan was very anxious about an assignment Mr. Larson had given the class. Everyone was going to have to give a speech about a book, but Ryan had never given a speech before. Ryan's sister, Tracey, asked him what was wrong.

"I've never given a presentation before," Ryan explained. "I have no idea how to do it."

Tracey said, "Everybody gets nervous before a presentation. But you can do it. First, you need to write what you want to say. Then, practice until you really know it. You can even practice in front of someone, to be sure you are definitely ready."

"I guess I could try doing it that way," Ryan said doubtfully. But, Ryan took his sister's advice and wrote his speech on notecards before practicing it by himself. After he practiced it five times, he practiced in front of Tracey. Tracey assured Ryan that his speech sounded great. Ryan arrived at school the day of his speech feeling nervous, but much more confident.

1. Who is the main character?
   - (A) Tracey
   - (B) Mr. Larson
   - (C) Ryan
   - (D) Ryan's father

2. Which part of speech is the word *nervous*?
   - (A) noun
   - (B) adverb
   - (C) verb
   - (D) adjective

3. What does the word *doubtfully* tell the reader in the last paragraph?
   - (A) Ryan is not sure whether Tracy is right.
   - (B) Ryan really wants to make a speech.
   - (C) Ryan is angry with Tracey.
   - (D) Ryan is convinced that Tracey is right.

Directions: Read the text, and answer the questions.

Shopping Malls

When was the last time you visited the mall? Malls can be very convenient places to shop and relax. You can purchase clothes, shoes, books, and computers all in the same place. Malls often have many interesting restaurants, too.

Most malls have large department stores called *anchor stores*. Anchor stores are the main stores in the mall. However, malls also have smaller stores that usually carry one type of product. For example, jewelry stores, video-game stores, and gift shops are smaller stores that are often in malls.

Malls often have a variety of kiosks (KEE-osks), too. Kiosks are small stands, usually placed in the middle of the mall. Kiosks sell many different things, such as hats, watches, or T-shirts. Many malls also have beauty salons and barbers; you can get your hair cut at the same place where you buy movies! Which stores are in your favorite mall?

1. Which word or phrase would tell a reader the most about this text?
   - (A) kiosks
   - (B) anchor stores
   - (C) gift shops
   - (D) malls

2. What are the main stores in many malls called?
   - (A) kiosks
   - (B) anchor stores
   - (C) malls
   - (D) gift shops

3. How does a kiosk relate to an anchor store?
   - (A) They are the same size.
   - (B) A kiosk is bigger.
   - (C) A kiosk is smaller.
   - (D) A kiosk is inside an anchor store.

4. Which word best describes malls?
   - (A) convenient
   - (B) tiny
   - (C) limited
   - (D) sharp

Directions: Write each word twice in cursive. Then, use it in a sentence.

1. horrible ______________________ ______________________

____

2. gullible ______________________ ______________________

____

3. tangible ______________________ ______________________

____

4. possible ______________________ ______________________

____

5. permissible ______________________ ______________________

____

6. invisible ______________________ ______________________

____

7. comprehensible ______________________ ______________________

____

8. eligible ______________________ ______________________

____

9. incredible ______________________ ______________________

____

Directions: Read and answer each question.

1. Circle the helping verb in the sentence.

   She may run for a second term.

2. Circle the linking verb in the sentence.

   Even with the cost of electricity, these cars are cheaper.

3. Circle the verbs in the sentence.

   Any ocean can be dangerous for people.

4. Circle the verbs in the sentence.

   If you join a group or a cause, you're jumping on the bandwagon.

5. Circle the helping verb in the sentence.

   Some people were kept on the island for a year.

6. Circle the linking verb in the sentence.

   Owls' powerful legs and sharp claws are perfect for hunting.

7. Circle the verb in the sentence.

   The eggs hatch into caterpillars.

8. Circle the linking verb in the sentence.

   There are only about 1,000 giant pandas left in the wild.

Directions: Read the facts about the *Orion* spacecraft. Then, think of a short narrative story you could write about *Orion*. Complete the graphic organizer with your ideas.

The Orion Spacecraft

- was designed to take astronauts into space to study asteroids and the planet Mars
- can carry up to four crew members
- is more powerful than any rocket ever built by NASA
- is currently in the testing phase of development

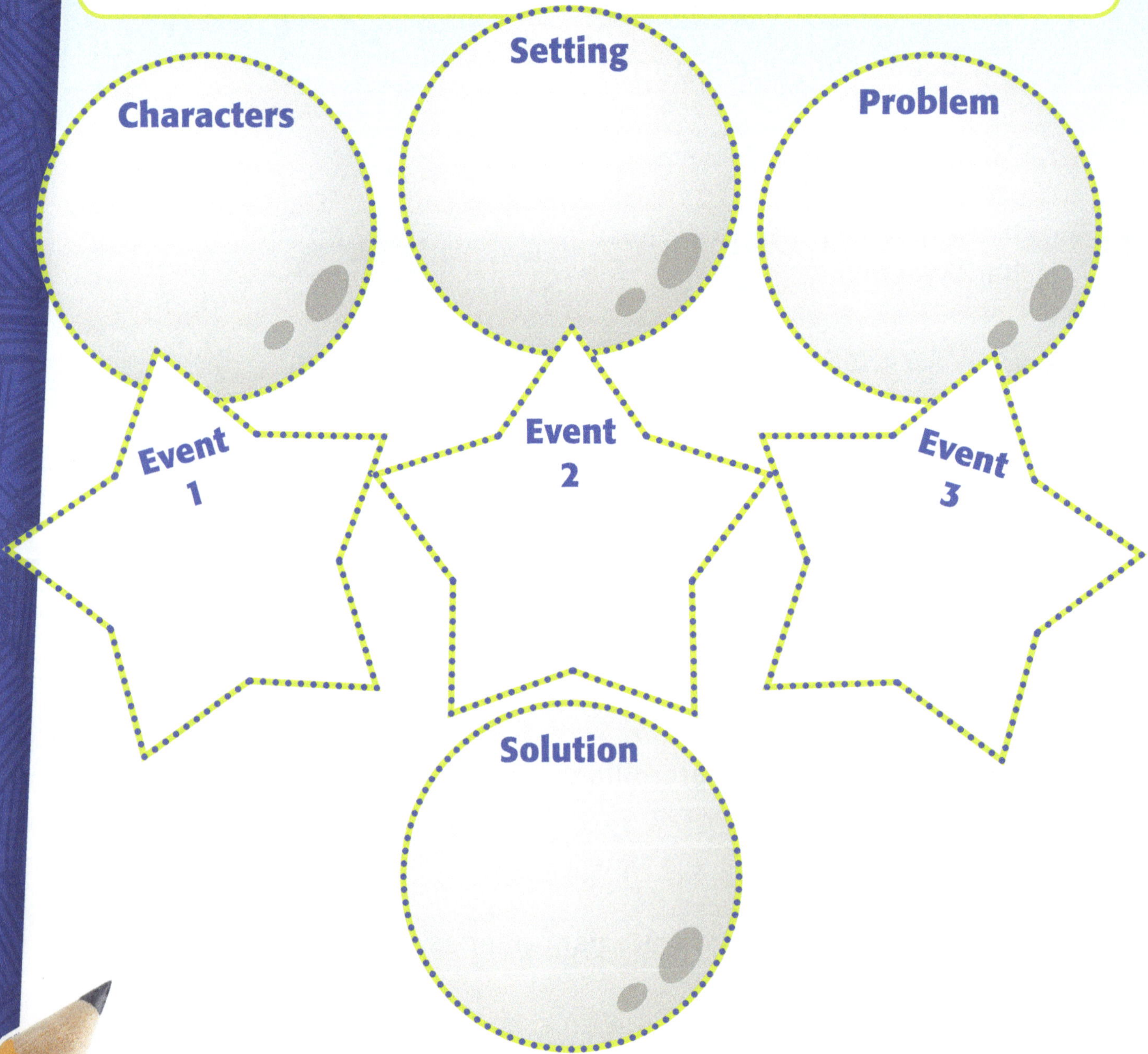

Directions: Imagine you are traveling on the *Orion*. Write a narrative about what the spacecraft is like. Include details about who you are on it with and what happens during your travels. Use the graphic organizer on page 56 to help you.

Remember

A strong narrative should:

- describe the setting
- include a problem or conflict
- explain how the problem or conflict was resolved

Directions: Solve each problem.

1. Calculate the perimeter of a rectangle that is 5 m by 3 m.

____

2. Calculate the perimeter of a square with 3 cm sides.

____

3. Calculate the perimeter of a rectangle that is 14 m by 27 m.

____

4. Calculate the perimeter of a rectangle that is 5.5 cm by 3.5 cm.

____

5. Calculate the perimeter of a square with 3.25 m sides.

____

6. Calculate the perimeter of an equilateral triangle with 6.5 cm sides.

____

7. Calculate the perimeter of a regular pentagon with 3 cm sides.

____

8. Calculate the perimeter of a regular hexagon with 4 cm sides.

____

9. Calculate the perimeter of a regular octagon with 2 cm sides.

____

10. Calculate the perimeter of a rectangle that is 1.75 m by 6.25 m.

____

Directions: Solve each problem.

1. What is the area of the polygon?

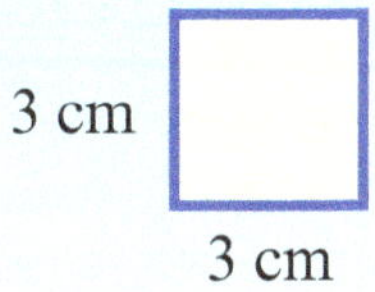

____

2. Calculate the area of a rectangle that is 5 m by 4 m.

____

3. What is the area of the polygon?

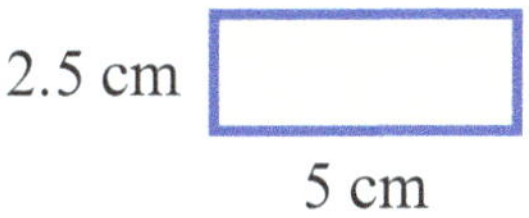

____

4. A rectangular garden has an area of 108 square meters. If its length is 18 m, what is its width?

____

5. What is the area of the polygon?

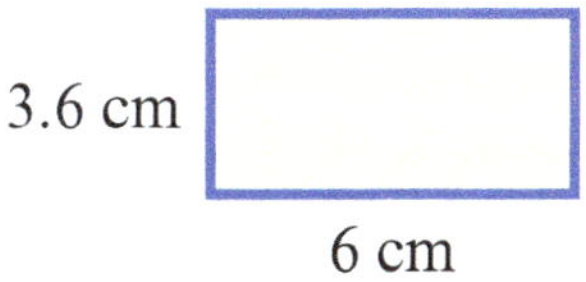

____

6. Calculate the area of a rectangle that is 14 cm by 3 cm.

____

7. What is the area of the square?

____

8. Calculate the area of a square that has 12 m sides.

____

9. What is the area of the polygon?

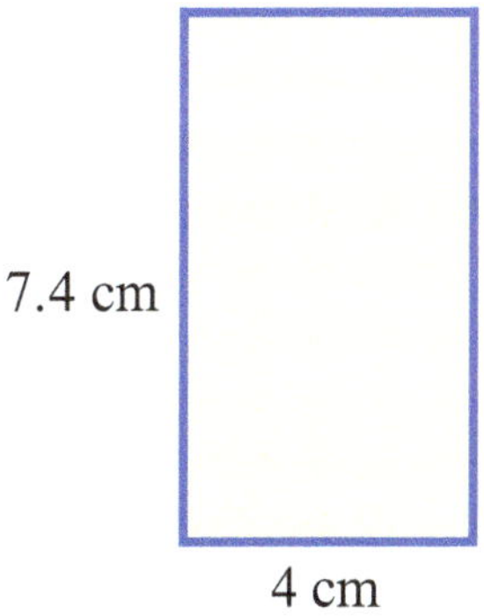

____

Directions: Look at the example. Then, solve the problem.

Problem 1: Find the volume of the figure.

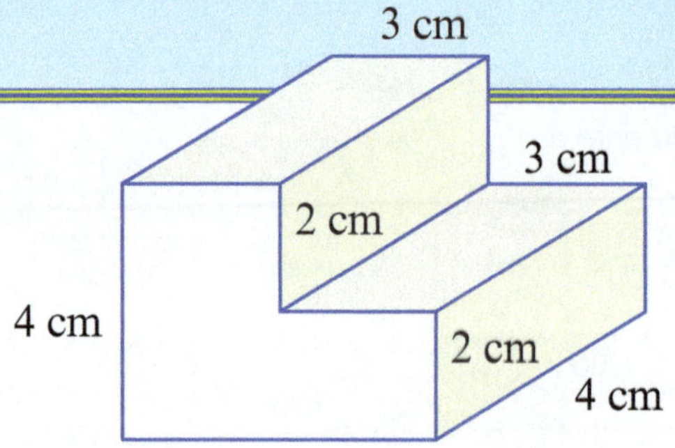

List What You Know	State Your Plan
Solve the Problem	**Look Back and Explain**

Problem 2: Find the volume of the figure.

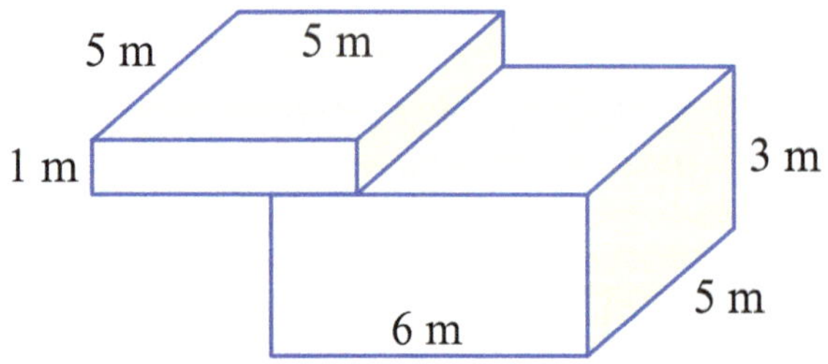

List What You Know	State Your Plan
Solve the Problem	**Look Back and Explain**

Directions: Look at the example. Then, solve the problem.

Example: Find the volume of the figure.

Figure	Prism 1 Dimensions and Volume	Prism 2 Dimensions and Volume	Total Volume
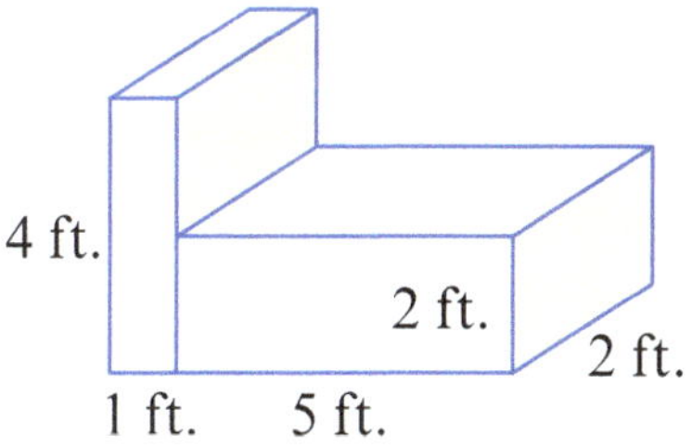	1 × 2 × 4 = 8 cubic feet	5 × 2 × 2 = 20 cubic feet	8 + 20 = 28 cubic feet

1. Find the volume of the figure.

Figure	Prism 1 Dimensions and Volume	Prism 2 Dimensions and Volume	Total Volume
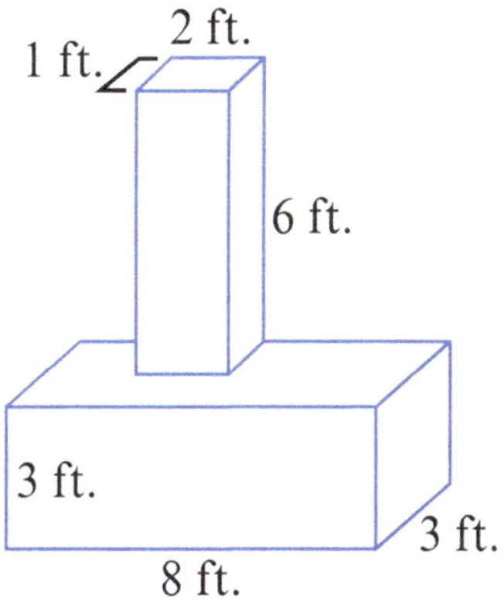			

2. Explain how you found the total volume of the figure.

____

____

____

____

Directions: Read the text, and answer the questions.

Taxes

The government provides goods and services to the public. For example, public libraries and public schools are provided by the government. Highways and road repairs are provided by the government, too. So, where does the money come from to pay for these things? It comes from taxes. We pay tax on products we buy. When people work, taxes are taken out of their paychecks. The money is used to pay for public services. It is also used to pay firefighters, police officers, and government leaders.

1. Where does tax money come from?

   ____

2. How are taxes used?

   ____

   ____

3. What goods and services have you used that were paid for with taxes?

   ____

   ____

4. Some people think that tax money should be spent on more programs that help people. Others think that taxes should be lowered so that people save money. What are the pros and cons of each perspective?

   ____

   ____

   ____

   ____

Directions: Follow the steps in the experiment to see how raw and cooked eggs are different.

What You Need

- raw egg
- gentle ramp
- hard-boiled egg
- plates
- newspaper
- notebook

What to Do

1. Hold the raw egg at the top of the ramp, and let it go. Then, do the same with the cooked egg. Record the results in your notebook.
2. Put a plate on a sheet of newspaper. Place a raw egg in the center of the plate. Make the egg spin.
3. Lightly place one finger on the spinning egg, then take your finger off. Record the results in your notebook.
4. Repeat steps 2 and 3 with the cooked egg.
5. What differences did you observe between the raw and the cooked eggs?

____

____

____

6. Why do you think the two eggs act differently?

____

____

____

Directions: Continue the following pattern.

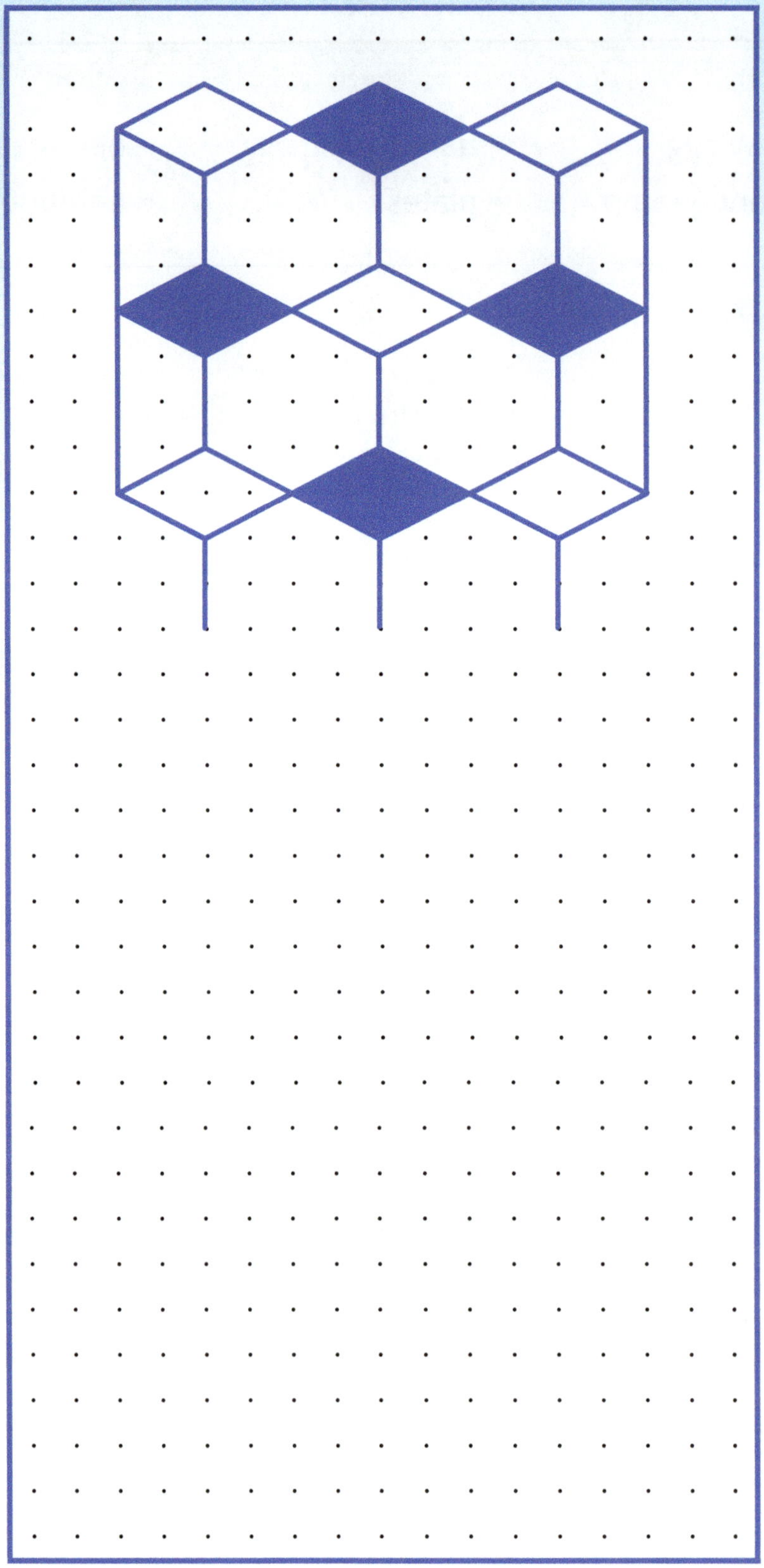

Directions: For this game, you will need 25 note cards and some colored markers, crayons, or pencils. On each card, write one of the words or phrases listed below using the specified color. On the back of each card, color a matching dot.

Red: the, your, my, his, her

Orange: monkey, octopus, shoes, beans, homework

Yellow: ate, squeezed, played with, cooked, sang for

Green: the toothpaste, a gopher, my socks, your dinner, an aardvark

Blue: at the kitchen table, behind a trash can, during a full moon, in the mud, while singing an opera

Directions: Shuffle the cards, and lay them dot side up in 5 rows of 5 cards each. Take turns choosing one card of each color. Then, flip them over, and arrange them to make a silly sentence! The player with the silliest sentence is the winner.

Spelling Activity

Write the spelling words from page 54 in brightly colored markers. Write each word in a different color.

Writing Activity

Research the *Orion* spacecraft. Revise your writing on page 57 to include three details you learned from your research.

Mathematics Activity

Choose two of the perimeter or area problems from pages 58–59. Explain to a family member how you solved the problems.

Problem-Solving Activity

Create a problem about the volume of a figure. Solve the problem, and then show a family member how you solved it.

Social Studies Activity

Imagine that you are in charge of your city or town. How would you spend the citizens' tax money? Why? Write a paragraph to explain your plan.

Listening-and-Speaking Activity

Explain to your family members all of the things that are paid for with their taxes.

Directions: Read the text, and answer the questions.

The Computer

Nicole and her brother were happy that their mom had decided to consider getting a new computer. They were both tired of sharing the computer that the family already had. Nicole asked her mom what kind of computer they were going to purchase.

"Before we decide that," her mom answered, "we need to decide what we want the computer to do. Once we figure that out, we'll have a better idea of the kind of computer we want."

"Maybe we should make a list of things we want," Nicole said. "Then, we can use that list to choose a computer."

"That makes a lot of sense," her mom said. "Let's start making that list." Before long, the family had a list of features they wanted in their new computer.

1. Which question would best help you monitor your reading?
   - (A) How old is Nicole?
   - (B) What other electronics does this family own?
   - (C) How will the family decide what computer to get?
   - (D) What is Nicole's brother's name?

2. Which is a clue that this text is fiction?
   - (A) rhyme
   - (B) dialogue
   - (C) imaginary creatures
   - (D) facts and dates

3. Which is a prepositional phrase?
   - (A) before we decide
   - (B) make a list
   - (C) going to purchase
   - (D) were both tired

4. Which is a synonym for *choose*?
   - (A) pick out
   - (B) pluck
   - (C) indecisive
   - (D) pull

Directions: Read the text, and answer the questions.

The Kalahari Desert

The Kalahari Desert spans three African countries; it goes across Botswana, Namibia, and South Africa. The Kalahari Desert is a very special place. Like other deserts, it is sandy and can get dry and very hot. But the Kalahari is not just sand dunes. There are also some woodlands and some dry grasslands. The Kalahari Desert does get some rainfall. When the summer rains come, flowers and plants bloom, and watering holes fill up.

Many different kinds of animals live in the Kalahari. When it is very hot and dry, these animals find ways to stay cool. When it rains, they go to the watering holes to drink.

1. On which continent would you find the Kalahari Desert?
   - (A) Asia
   - (B) Africa
   - (C) North America
   - (D) Australia

2. Which is not a fact about the Kalahari Desert?
   - (A) Many kinds of animals live there.
   - (B) It is a very large desert.
   - (C) It is in three countries.
   - (D) It has only sand dunes.

3. What does the word *spans* mean?
   - (A) goes across
   - (B) is hot
   - (C) rains
   - (D) goes under

4. What is this text mostly about?
   - (A) the Kalahari Desert
   - (B) woodlands and grasslands
   - (C) rain
   - (D) the seasons

Directions: A superlative is the most extreme. For example, that ladybug might be *tiny*, but this one is the *tiniest*. *Tiniest* is a superlative. Write the root word and the superlative of each word. An example has been done for you.

1. great ____ greater ____ greatest
2. ____________ higher ____________
3. ____________ heavier ____________
4. ____________ noisier ____________
5. ____________ farther ____________
6. ____________ bigger ____________
7. ____________ closer ____________
8. ____________ angrier ____________
9. ____________ brighter ____________
10. ____________ busier ____________

Directions: Write a few sentences using superlatives.

____

____

____

____

____

____

Directions: Circle the conjunction in each sentence.

1. He was called a forester and an outlaw.

2. Sneeze or cough into your elbow.

3. Listeners thought the invasion was real, and thousands of people panicked.

4. It would be great if you could grow your own money!

5. Nickel is a metal, but the coin wasn't all nickel.

6. Radar helps, too, because it shows where the birds are.

7. You can foster a dog or a cat for a while.

8. Gold can be melted down and made into new things.

9. It's hard to match red and orange together.

10. I love to dance, so I wore a tutu.

Directions: Circle the statements below that could be included in an informative/explanatory paragraph about Amelia Earhart.

I think it was very interesting that Amelia Earhart and Eleanor Roosevelt were friends.

Earhart always looked very stylish in her flying uniforms.

Earhart attended different flying schools.

The United States spent $4 million trying to find Earhart after her plane went missing.

Earhart disappeared in 1937 while flying around the world.

Earhart was the 16th woman to receive a pilot's license.

I believe aliens abducted Earhart, and that is why no one has found her.

Earhart should have never tried to fly around the world.

Directions: Write an informative/explanatory paragraph about Amelia Earhart's last flight. Include details about where the flight took place and what happened after she disappeared. Use the graphic organizer on page 71 to help you.

Remember!

A strong informative/explanatory paragraph should:

- open with a hook to grab the reader's attention
- include details and facts
- end with a strong conclusion

Directions: Solve each problem.

1. Name the shape that is created by the cross-section.

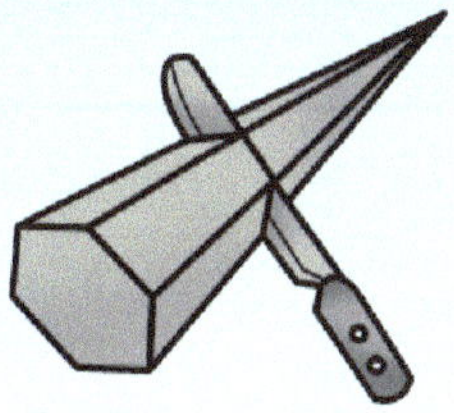

2. Are there any perpendicular lines in the letter T?

3. Are the angles inside a regular octagon *acute*, *right*, or *obtuse*?

4. Name the triangle that has 3 unequal sides.

5. Name this polygon.

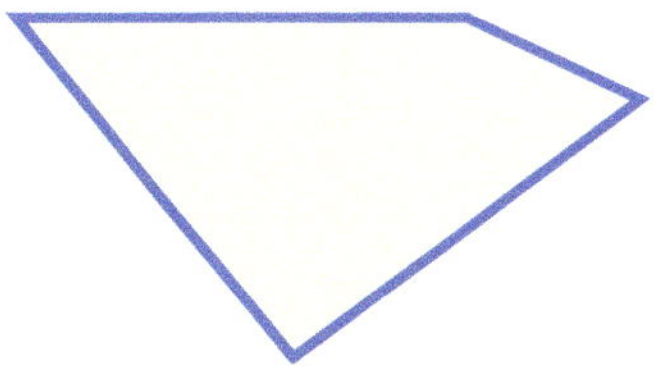

6. Name the quadrilateral with one set of parallel sides.

7. Does a regular hexagon have any parallel lines?

8. Are these triangles congruent?

9. Does a triangle have any parallel lines?

10. How many degrees are in a straight line?

Directions: Solve each problem.

1. Draw at least 2 lines of symmetry.

2. How many lines of symmetry could be drawn in the square above?

____

3. How many lines of symmetry does this triangle have?

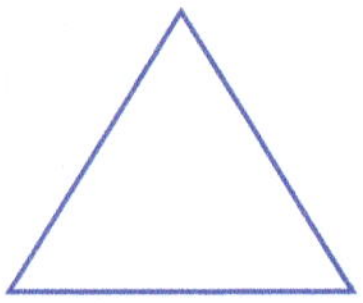

____

4. Draw all the lines of symmetry.

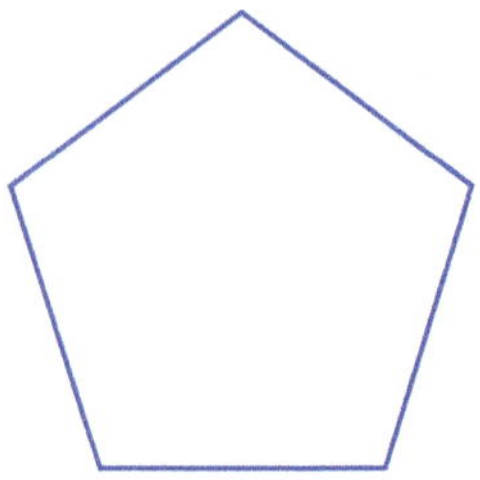

5. How many lines of symmetry does this rectangle have?

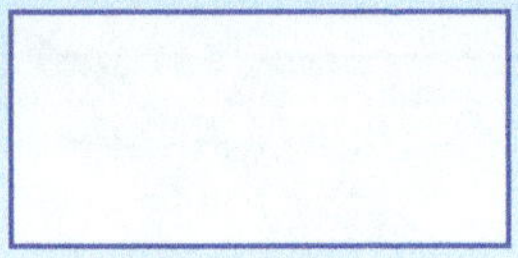

____

6. How many lines of symmetry does a regular octagon have?

____

7. How many lines of symmetry does this triangle have?

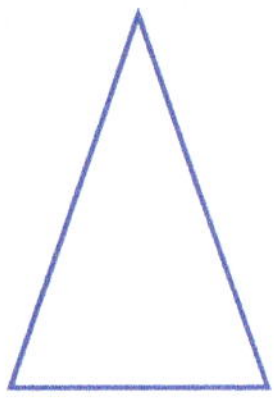

____

8. How many lines of symmetry does this polygon have?

____

Directions: Read and solve each problem.

Problem 1: Carol works at a cosmetics counter at a department store. She counts the perfume bottles and records the results on a line plot. How many bottles of perfume does Carol count?

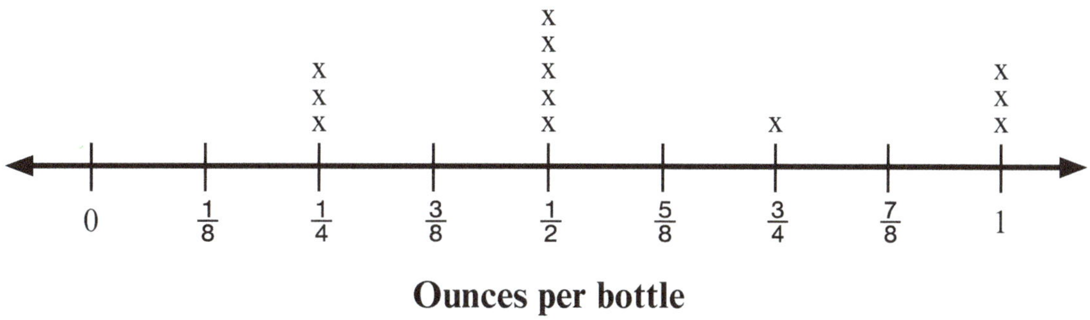

List What You Know	State Your Plan
Solve the Problem	**Look Back and Explain**

Problem 2: Carol wants to know how many ounces of perfume are in all of the bottles combined. Use the line plot from problem 1 to find the answer.

List What You Know	State Your Plan
Solve the Problem	**Look Back and Explain**

Directions: Look at the example. Then, solve the problem.

Example: Brett is a chef at a restaurant. He counts the bottles of each spice and writes the number of ounces in each bottle. Make a line plot with the data.

Spice	Number of Bottles	Bottle Size
Italian seasoning	3	$\frac{3}{4}$ ounce
dried chives	1	$\frac{1}{8}$ ounce
rosemary leaves	1	$\frac{3}{8}$ ounce
parsley flakes	2	$\frac{1}{4}$ ounce
basil leaves	3	$\frac{1}{2}$ ounce

Restaurant Spice Rack Inventory

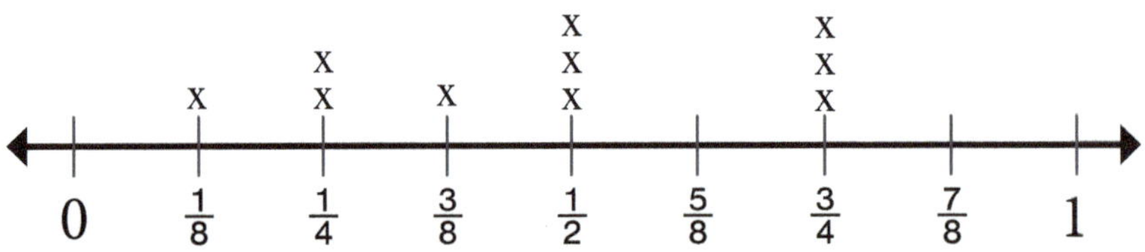

Ounces per bottle

Saul works at a bakery. He counts the bottles of each spice and writes the number of ounces in each bottle. Make a line plot with the data.

Spice	Number of Bottles	Bottle Size
cinnamon	3	$4\frac{1}{8}$ ounces
ginger	2	$4\frac{1}{2}$ ounces
orange peel	1	5 ounces
vanilla extract	1	4 ounces
nutmeg	2	$4\frac{3}{4}$ ounces

Title: ______________________________

____

Directions: Read the text, and answer the questions.

Currencies

Different countries use different currencies, or types of money. The United States uses the dollar. Mexico uses the peso. Many countries in Europe use the euro. Certain kinds of money have greater value than others. For example, a U.S. dollar might be worth 19 Mexican pesos. This is called the *exchange rate*. Exchange rates change all the time.

Do an online search for "currency exchange calculator." Select your country's currency. Then, compare it to the currencies below. If the rate is less than 1, it means that the other country's currency is worth more. If the rate is more than 1, it means that your country's currency is worth more.

American dollar

____

Australian dollar

____

Belgian franc

____

euro

____

Greek drachma

____

Japanese yen

____

Pakistani rupee

____

Swedish krona

____

1. Which currency is worth the most? Which is worth the least?

____

____

Directions: Follow the steps in this experiment to discover what an electromagnet is.

What You Need

- copper wire
- long steel screw
- metal paper clips
- 9-volt battery
- C battery
- tape

What to Do

1. Wrap the copper wire around the screw just once. Tape the ends to the C battery. You have made an electromagnet.
2. Touch the screw to a pile of paper clips. How many paper clips does the electromagnet pick up? ________________
3. Repeat steps 1 and 2 with different numbers of turns around the screw. Record your results. Then, repeat the experiment using a 9-volt battery.

Number of Turns	Number of Clips for a C Battery	Number of Clips for a 9-Volt Battery

4. What conclusion can you make regarding the strength of the electromagnet, the number of coils, and the voltage of the battery?

____

____

____

Directions: Think of something that fits each category, and write it on the line.

1. Something that makes me happy: ____________________
2. Something that can only be seen in the winter: ____________________
3. Something that can only be seen in the fall: ____________________
4. Something that can be found in a bathroom cabinet: ____________________
5. Something that drives me crazy: ____________________
6. Something that changes color: ____________________
7. Something I open: ____________________
8. Something I mix: ____________________
9. Something that has a key: ____________________
10. Something that changes shape: ____________________

Directions: Look at the items you wrote above. How else could you categorize these 10 things?

____

____

UNIT 5

Game

Directions: Play with a partner. Use small objects to mark your places. Roll one number cube. Move the number of spaces that you roll. If you land on a space with a word, say the word, its base word, and the superlative. The first player to reach the finish wins.

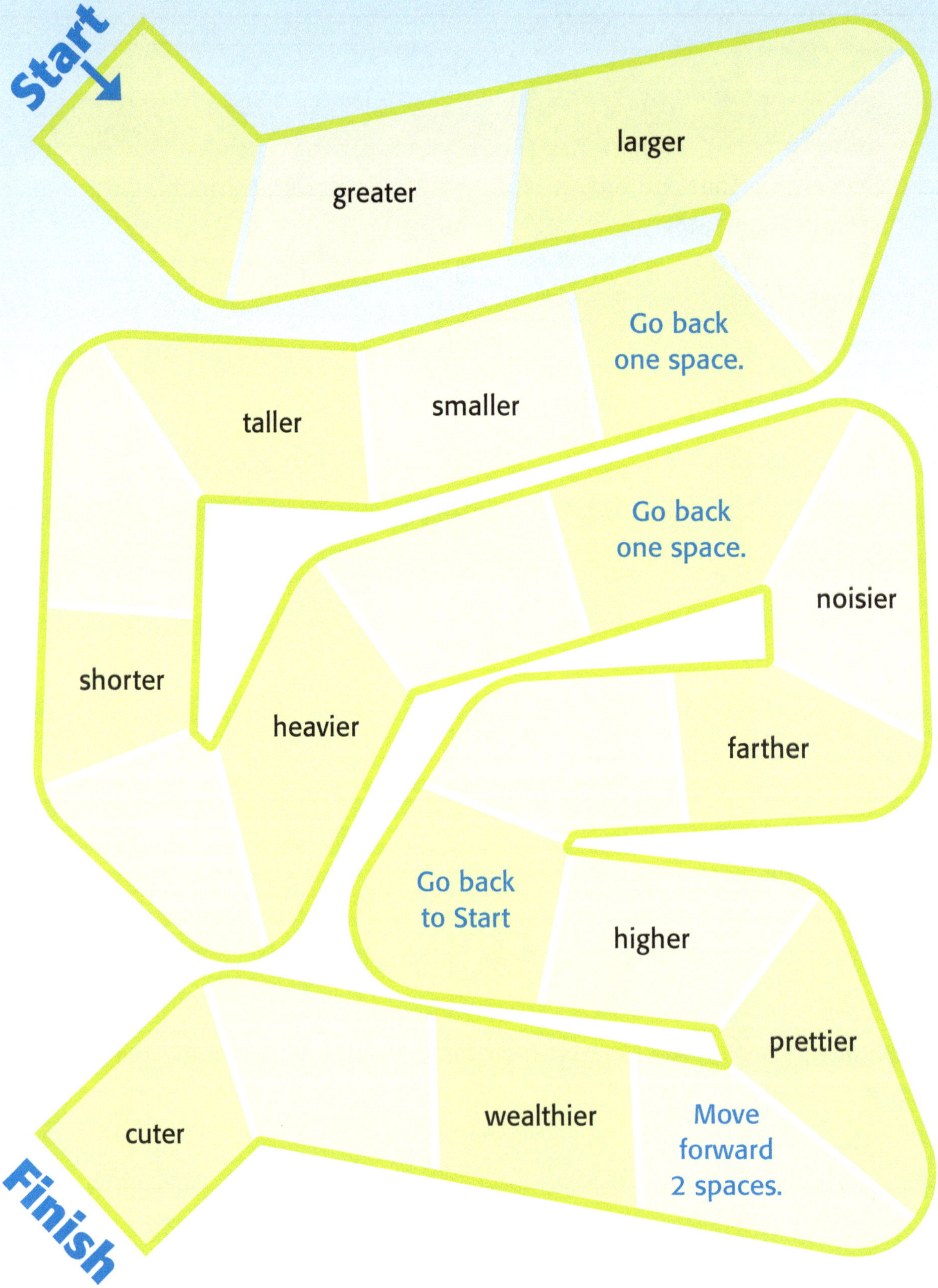

Spelling Activity

Write a series of sentences using superlatives. Example: *This kitten is fast. This kitten is faster. That kitten is the fastest.*

Writing Activity

Imagine you are a reporter in 1937, covering the disappearance of Amelia Earhart. Revise your paragraph on page 72 to include this perspective.

Mathematics Activity

Look through a magazine, and find five objects that are symmetrical. Identify their lines of symmetry.

Social Studies Activity

A particular video game in Germany costs 64 euros. How much would it cost in U.S. dollars?

Science Activity

Review your experiment from page 78. Wrap the screw in aluminum foil, and repeat the experiment. How does this affect your results?

Listening-and-Speaking Activity

Give a speech to your family about different currencies used around the world. Explain how their values compare to your country's currency.

Directions: Read the text, and answer the questions on the next page.

The Summer Olympic Games

Every four years, a very special event occurs. Athletes from all over the world gather to compete in different sports. They try to win medals. That special event is called the Summer Olympic Games. It is also called the Olympiad. Many sports are a part of the Olympics. Athletes row, fence, and ride horses. They swim, run, and play soccer. Judo and boxing are also part of the Summer Olympics. So are baseball and gymnastics.

How did the Olympics start? Nearly 3,000 years ago in ancient Greece, people got together every four years. They raced and boxed. They competed to see who could throw a spear the farthest. There were other events, too. After many years, the Greeks stopped having the games. For a long time, there were no games. Then in 1896, the modern Olympics began. The first modern Olympic Games were held in Athens. Athens is the capital of Greece. Since 1900, the games have been held every four years. The games have only been cancelled three times—in 1916, 1940, and 1944. In those years, the games could not be held because of World War I and World War II.

Where are the Olympics held? Each Olympiad is held in a different city. Cities that want to host the Olympics apply to have the Games. They apply to a group of people called the International Olympic Committee. This group decides which city will host the Games. The Games have been held in cities all over the world. They have been held in Paris, France and Los Angeles, California. Rome, Italy and Tokyo, Japan have also hosted the Games. The Olympics have been held in many other places, too. In 2016, the Games were held in Rio de Janeiro, Brazil. Wherever the Summer Games are held, millions of people will be watching them.

Directions: Read "The Summer Olympic Games," and then answer the questions.

1. Which event happens first?
   - (A) Cities apply to the International Olympic Committee.
   - (B) Cities decide that they want to host the Olympic Games.
   - (C) The Olympics are held.
   - (D) The committee decides where the Olympics will be.

2. Why were the first modern Olympic Games held in Athens?
   - (A) The Olympics began in Greece.
   - (B) Athens was the largest city in the world.
   - (C) Athens had the most athletes.
   - (D) No other city wanted to have the Olympics.

3. What is a good reason to read this text?
   - (A) to learn about the Olympics
   - (B) to travel to London
   - (C) to learn about ancient Greece
   - (D) to learn how to row

4. What is most likely the author's opinion?
   - (A) People should not compete in the Olympic Games.
   - (B) The Olympic Games are too dangerous for athletes.
   - (C) The Olympic Games are exciting.
   - (D) The Olympic Games are boring.

5. Which sentence reflects a main idea of the text?
   - (A) The Olympics have been played for many years.
   - (B) They apply to a special group of people.
   - (C) They swim, run, and play soccer.
   - (D) They try to win medals.

6. What is this text mostly about?
   - (A) Tokyo
   - (B) the Olympics
   - (C) Greece
   - (D) games

Directions: Double the final consonant and add *–ing* to each word. Then, write a sentence using one of the words.

1. strap ______________________
2. begin ______________________
3. stop ______________________
4. skip ______________________
5. expel ______________________
6. transfer ______________________
7. equip ______________________
8. regret ______________________
9. prefer ______________________
10. occur ______________________

____

____

____

____

____

Directions: Circle the prepositional phrases in these sentences.

1. By the 1800s, people realized cleanliness was important.

2. The workers set a new record for laying track.

3. In 2014, an outbreak of the disease made people very nervous.

4. He became famous for his funny limericks.

5. Senator Nelson thought about pollution often.

6. Some monkeys crack nuts with stones.

7. All new laws must be signed by the president.

8. The ancient Romans built sewer systems in the city.

9. The well sat on top of the hill.

10. What is that strange shape over there behind that door?

Directions: Read each fact about President Abraham Lincoln. Then, write your opinion about the topic and Lincoln.

Topic: United States of America

Fact: Lincoln did not want the country to split apart over slavery. He wanted to keep the Union together. He said, "A house divided against itself cannot stand."

My Opinion: ____

____

____

Topic: Slavery

Fact: Lincoln did not believe in slavery. He did not want it to spread to the new states.

My Opinion: ____

____

____

Topic: The Civil War

Fact: Lincoln made General Ulysses S. Grant the commander of the Union Army. Grant helped the North win the Civil War. Lincoln had succeeded in keeping the Union together.

My Opinion: ____

____

____

Directions: Do you think Abraham Lincoln was a good president? Write an opinion paragraph about him. Include reasons why you do or do not think he was a good president. Use your notes on page 86 to help you.

Edit and Revise!

Be sure to check your writing for:

- a clearly stated opinion
- reasons and details that support your opinion
- logically ordered thoughts on the topic

Directions: Solve each problem.

1. Is the angle *obtuse*, *acute*, or *right*?

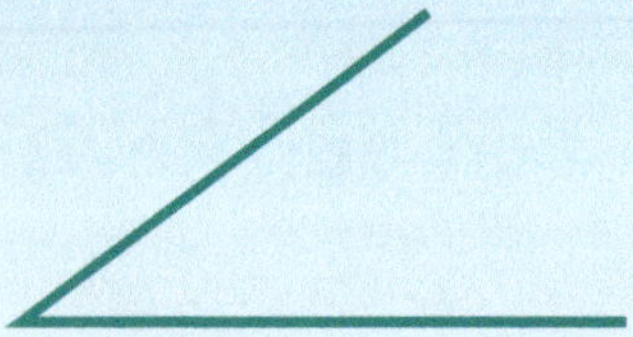

____

2. True or false? A hexagon has six right angles.

____

3. Circle the acute angles in this polygon.

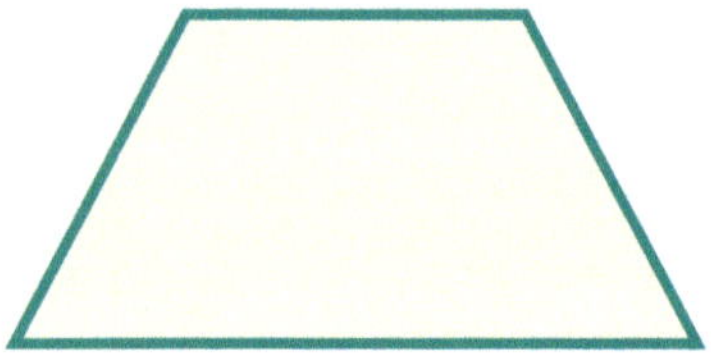

4. How many angles are inside a pentagon?

____

5. Is the angle *obtuse, acute,* or *right?*

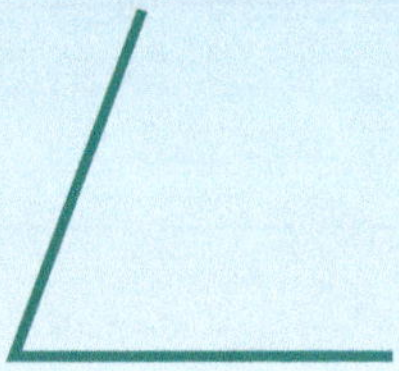

____

6. What type of triangle has one 90° angle?

____

7. Is the angle *obtuse, acute* or *right*?

____

8. Is the angle below greater than, less than, or equal to 90°?

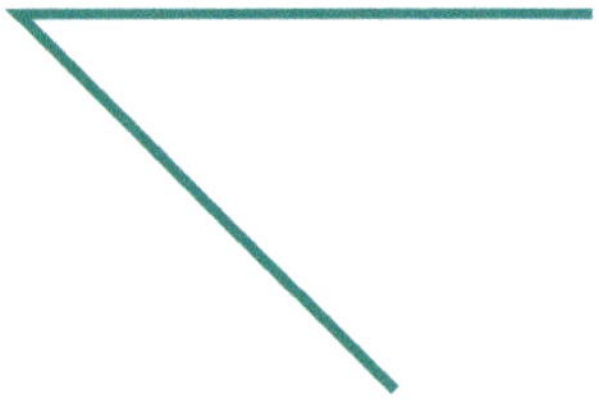

____

Directions: Solve each problem.

1. Use a protractor to measure the angle.

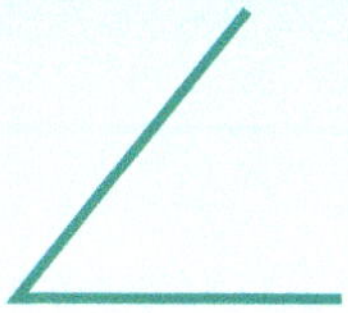

2. Use a protractor to measure the angle.

3. Use a protractor to measure the angle.

4. Which measurement is the angle below most likely to be: 70°, 90°, or 110°?

5. Is the angle right, obtuse, or acute?

6. Is the angle below closest to: 40°, 70°, or 90°?

7. Use a protractor to draw an acute angle.

8. Use a protractor to draw an obtuse angle.

Directions: Read and solve the problem.

Nadia goes on a bike-riding tour. She rides 15 miles in 6 hours. She rides the same distance each hour. How far does she ride in one hour? Remember, there are 5,280 feet in 1 mile.

1. Solve the problem by showing your answer in miles.

2. Solve the problem by showing your answer in miles and feet.

3. Solve the problem by showing your answer in feet.

Directions: Read and solve the problem.

Some jellyfish are only 0.018 meters wide. However, a lion's mane jellyfish can be 1.8 meters wide. How many times wider is the lion's mane jellyfish?

1. Draw a model to show how many times greater the digit 1 is in 1.8 than in 0.018.

2. Draw a model to show how many times greater the digit 8 is in 1.8 than in 0.018.

3. How many times wider is the lion's mane jellyfish? Show how you found your answer.

Directions: Read the text, and answer the questions.

The United Nations

The United Nations (also called the UN) was established at the end of World War II. War-torn countries wanted peace in the world. So, they formed the United Nations as a way to cooperate and work with one another. Countries in the United Nations are called Member States. As of 2016, there were 193 Member States. The UN focuses on issues that involve the whole world. It focuses on world peace and safety. It focuses on climate change, terrorism, and health emergencies. The United Nations also focuses on food production and human rights.

1. Why was the United Nations formed?

____

____

2. What does the United Nations do?

____

____

____

3. What issues can you think of that affect the whole world?

____

____

____

____

Directions: Follow the steps in this experiment to see how strong air is.

What You Need

- paper
- clear plastic jar
- bowl of water

What to Do

1. Scrunch up the paper very tightly.
2. Squash it into the bottom of the jar so that when you turn the jar upside down, the paper does not fall out.
3. Turn the jar upside down. Keeping it straight, lower it into the bowl of water. Does the paper get wet?

   ____

4. Write and draw to show what you have done. Explain what the water, the paper, and the air inside the jar were doing.

UNIT 6

Critical Thinking

Directions: Write a story problem that has an answer of 56. Draw a picture or a model to represent the problem. Give the problem to someone else, but don't tell him or her the answer!

Directions: Write these words on index cards, or make a copy of this page and cut the words out. Shuffle the cards. Take turns with a partner selecting a card, reading the word, and then naming the appropriate rule for adding *–ing*. Keep playing until all the cards have been used.

Adding *-ing*

- **Rule 1**: When a short-vowel word ends in a single consonant, double the consonant and add *–ing*.
- **Rule 2**: If a word ends in silent *e*, drop the *e* and add *–ing*.
- **Rule 3**: When a long-vowel word ends in a consonant, just add *–ing*.
- **Rule 4**: When a short-vowel word ends in a double consonant, just add *–ing*.

tape	give	mash
fill	relate	rain
transport	convert	prepare
break	camp	slip
miss	grab	make
transmit	live	click
overlap	derail	mark

Spelling Activity

Write the spelling words from page 84 in printing and in cursive.

Writing Activity

Read your paragraph on page 87 out loud to yourself. Pay attention to any grammatical errors or parts of the writing that do not flow smoothly. Make revisions as needed.

Mathematics Activity

Find something in your house that has a 90 degree angle. Find something that has a 45 degree angle. Find something that has an obtuse angle.

Social Studies Activity

Research the requirements to join the United Nations. Why aren't all countries allowed to join?

Science Activity

Research a diving bell. How is this similar to and different from the experiment you did on page 93?

Listening-and-Speaking Activity

Explain the United Nations to a family member. Encourage him or her to ask questions. Answer to the best of your ability.

Directions: Read the text, and answer the questions on the next page.

Common Ground

Katie's father was at the airport waiting to meet her. She was going to spend a week with him, and usually she really enjoyed their visits. But this time was different; her dad was getting married, and Katie wasn't at all sure she liked the idea.

On the way from the airport to her dad's house, Katie didn't say very much. Finally, her dad asked, "Do you want to talk about it, Katie?"

For a moment, Katie sat silently. Then, she said, "I'm sorry, Dad, I just don't think I want you to get married."

"I thought you liked Celia," Katie's dad said.

"I do like Celia," Katie answered. "It's not that at all. I just don't know if I want her for a stepmother—that's totally different."

"It really is different," her dad agreed. "But I hope you'll get to like having Celia as a stepmother. She likes you an awful lot, you know, and I'll bet Megan will, too."

"Who's Megan?" Katie asked. She hadn't heard that name before.

"She's Celia's daughter," her dad responded. "She's your age, actually, so maybe you'll even have some things in common."

After dropping Katie's luggage off at her dad's house, Katie and her dad went to meet Celia and Megan at a restaurant. They were going to have dinner together. When they got to the restaurant, Celia and Megan were already there. Celia introduced Megan to Katie. At first, Katie didn't know what to say to Megan. But then, Megan said, "Mom, don't forget I have swimming practice tomorrow."

"You like to swim?" Katie asked hopefully.

"I love it—I'm on our school's swim team," Megan answered excitedly. "Do you swim?"

"I love to swim, too," Katie said with a smile. Maybe having Celia as a stepmother wasn't going to be so bad after all.

Directions: Read "Common Ground," and then answer the questions.

1. At the beginning of the story, how does Katie feel about her dad getting married?
   - (A) excited
   - (B) unhappy
   - (C) overjoyed
   - (D) unaware

2. What makes Katie change her mind about having Celia for a stepmother?
   - (A) Her dad and Celia get married.
   - (B) Her dad and Celia give her a gift.
   - (C) She finds out that Celia likes to swim.
   - (D) She finds out that Megan likes to swim.

3. Which question reflects an appropriate purpose for reading this text?
   - (A) What is Katie's big discovery?
   - (B) Why do Katie and her dad dislike each other so much?
   - (C) Where is Katie's mother?
   - (D) Is Katie afraid to fly in an airplane?

4. How does Katie's dad know that Katie has something on her mind?
   - (A) Katie yells at her dad.
   - (B) Katie won't get in the car with her dad.
   - (C) Katie doesn't say very much.
   - (D) Katie tells her dad she's angry with him.

5. How does Katie's dad likely feel now that Katie and Megan have something in common?
   - (A) angry
   - (B) afraid
   - (C) exhausted
   - (D) relieved

6. Which phrase lets the reader know that Katie will end up being happy?
   - (A) "I have swimming practice tomorrow."
   - (B) "I'm sorry, Dad."
   - (C) "I do like Celia."
   - (D) "…a stepmother wasn't going to be so bad after all."

Directions: The prefix *com–* means *with* or *together*. Write each word in printing and in cursive. Think about how the prefix affects each word's meaning.

1. communicate
2. comparison
3. combine
4. companion
5. committee
6. commission
7. completely
8. community
9. compete
10. common

Directions: Circle the proper nouns in these sentences.

1. Leo B. Hart established a school for the children.

2. Sitting Bull and Crazy Horse led warriors in a fight to save their land.

3. The museums and the National Zoo are free.

4. He created a clown character called Bip.

5. Top athletes compete in the Paralympic Games.

6. The adoration for the Beatles was called *Beatlemania*.

7. The locomotive is owned by the Smithsonian Institution.

8. He announced that the Greeks had won a battle.

9. Saad wasn't happy with how Susan treated him at the store.

10. Most Americans stand to say the Pledge of Allegiance.

Directions: Imagine you are trapped in a blizzard. There is snow everywhere, and you are the coldest you have ever been. Add sensory details to the graphic organizer to describe the experience.

I see…

I smell…

I feel…

I hear…

I taste…

Directions: Imagine you are trapped in a blizzard. Write a narrative describing your experience. Use your notes on page 101 to help you.

Edit and Revise!

Be sure to check that your writing:

- is very descriptive
- includes sensory details
- paints a picture with words for the reader

Directions: Solve each problem.

1. Complete the input/output table. Look for a pattern, and write the rule.

Input	1	2	3	4	5	6
Output	6	12				

____

2. Sherri pays $4.50 for 25 trading cards. What is the cost of each card?

____

3. There are 6 balls. Half of the balls are blue. One ball is red. The rest are green. What fraction of the balls are green?

____

4. Complete the input/output table. Look for a pattern, and write the rule.

Input	1	2	3	4	5	6
Output	4	8				

____

5. A class of 25 students is making necklaces. The necklaces each have 30 beads. How many beads are needed for each student to make one necklace?

____

6. Nicole has five times as many stickers in her sticker collection as her sister. Her sister has 32 stickers. How many stickers does Nicole have?

____

7. Mitch dog-sits for the family next door. They pay him $3.00 per day. If they go on vacation for 2 weeks, how much money will Mitch earn?

____

8. Jackie left home at 3:15. She spent 15 minutes walking to the movie theater. The movie lasted $2\frac{1}{2}$ hours. Then, she walked home. What time did she arrive back home?

____

Directions: Solve each problem.

1. Harry wants to buy an MP3 player that costs $46.94. He has $10.25 in his piggy bank. He gets $4.25 for allowance each week. How many weeks will he need to save to have enough money for the MP3 player?

____

2. A box of trading cards costs $5.50. Michael wants to purchase 3 boxes. How much money does Michael need?

____

3. Mom bought 3 pounds of bananas at the store. The bananas cost 89 cents a pound. If she paid for the bananas with a five dollar bill, how much change did she get back?

____

4. A magazine costs $3.25. If you buy one each week, how much money will you spend in 2 months?

____

5. Marcia is making ice cream sundaes. She has vanilla ice cream, sprinkles, whipped cream, and cherries. How many different types of ice cream sundaes can she make?

____

6. There can be 72 students in each grade at Miller School. The fifth grade has 3 teachers. Mrs. Shaw's class has 21 students. Mr. Brown's class has 23 students. Mrs. Ralley's class has 23 students. How many more students can enroll in fifth grade?

____

Directions: Read and solve the problem.

Valerie is making salsa using a recipe that makes 12 servings. After chopping up some fresh tomatoes, she adds the ingredients shown.

Salsa Recipe

- $\frac{1}{2}$ cup fresh cilantro
- $\frac{1}{4}$ cup fresh chopped onion
- $\frac{1}{3}$ cup lime juice
- $\frac{1}{6}$ cup minced garlic

1. Draw pictures to show the fraction of the ingredients that are in each serving of salsa.

2. Write equations to show the fraction of the ingredients that are in each serving of salsa.

3. If Valerie makes 10 servings of salsa using the same amount of each ingredient, would each serving have more or less of each ingredient? Explain your thinking.

____

____

____

Directions: Read and solve the problem.

Evaluate each expression. Then, determine which expressions are less than 0.8, equal to 0.8, or greater than 0.8.

8×10^1	0.8×10^1	0.08×10^2	0.08×10^3
$80 \div 10^1$	$80 \div 10^3$	0.008×10^1	0.008×10^3
$0.8 \div 10^1$	0.8×10^2	$800 \div 10^2$	$800 \div 10^3$

1. Write the expressions in the correct section of the table.

Less than 0.8	Equal to 0.8	Greater than 0.8

2. What helped you determine where to write each expression?

____

____

____

Directions: Read the text, and answer the questions.

The Environment

The environment is affected by the entire world population. This is known as the global environment. The Industrial Revolution had negative effects on the global environment. It was a time when large factories increased in number. More fuel was used, and large cities grew even larger. The large factories burned a lot of fuel. This polluted the air. Today, people know more about how we can affect the planet. But, there are more factories and people than ever before. We must always think of more ways we can reduce our impact. This will keep people healthy and safe.

1. How does population growth affect the environment?

____

____

2. How can people affect the environment?

____

____

3. What responsibility do we have to protect the environment?

____

____

4. What do you think you can do to help?

____

____

Directions: Follow the steps in this experiment to discover what a mixture is.

What You Need

- warm water
- 4 plastic cups
- sugar
- sand
- teaspoons
- strainer
- salt
- dirt

What to Do

1. Place about a teaspoon of salt in the first cup, sand in the second cup, sugar in the third cup, and dirt in the fourth cup.

2. Fill each cup halfway with warm water. Stir each mixture. Describe what happens to each cup.

   salt cup: ______________________

   sugar cup: ______________________

   sand cup: ______________________

   dirt cup: ______________________

3. Use the strainer to pour the liquid out of each cup. What is left over in the cups?

   salt cup: ______________________

   sugar cup: ______________________

   sand cup: ______________________

   dirt cup: ______________________

Directions: Camille, Marcello, Tyrell, and Stacy are all different ages (9, 11, 12, and 14). Use the clues to figure out how old each child is. Use symbols in the chart below to keep track of the information.

Camille's age is an odd number.

Tyrell is older than Camille.

Marcello's age is a prime number.

Stacy will be a teenager next year.

	9	11	12	14
Camille				
Marcello				
Tyrell				
Stacy				

Camille is ____________ Tyrell is ______________

Marcello is ___________ Stacy is ______________

Directions: Play with a partner. Use small objects to mark your places. Take turns rolling a number cube. Move the number of spaces that you roll. If you land on a space with words, say a fact and an opinion about the topic. The first player to the finish wins.

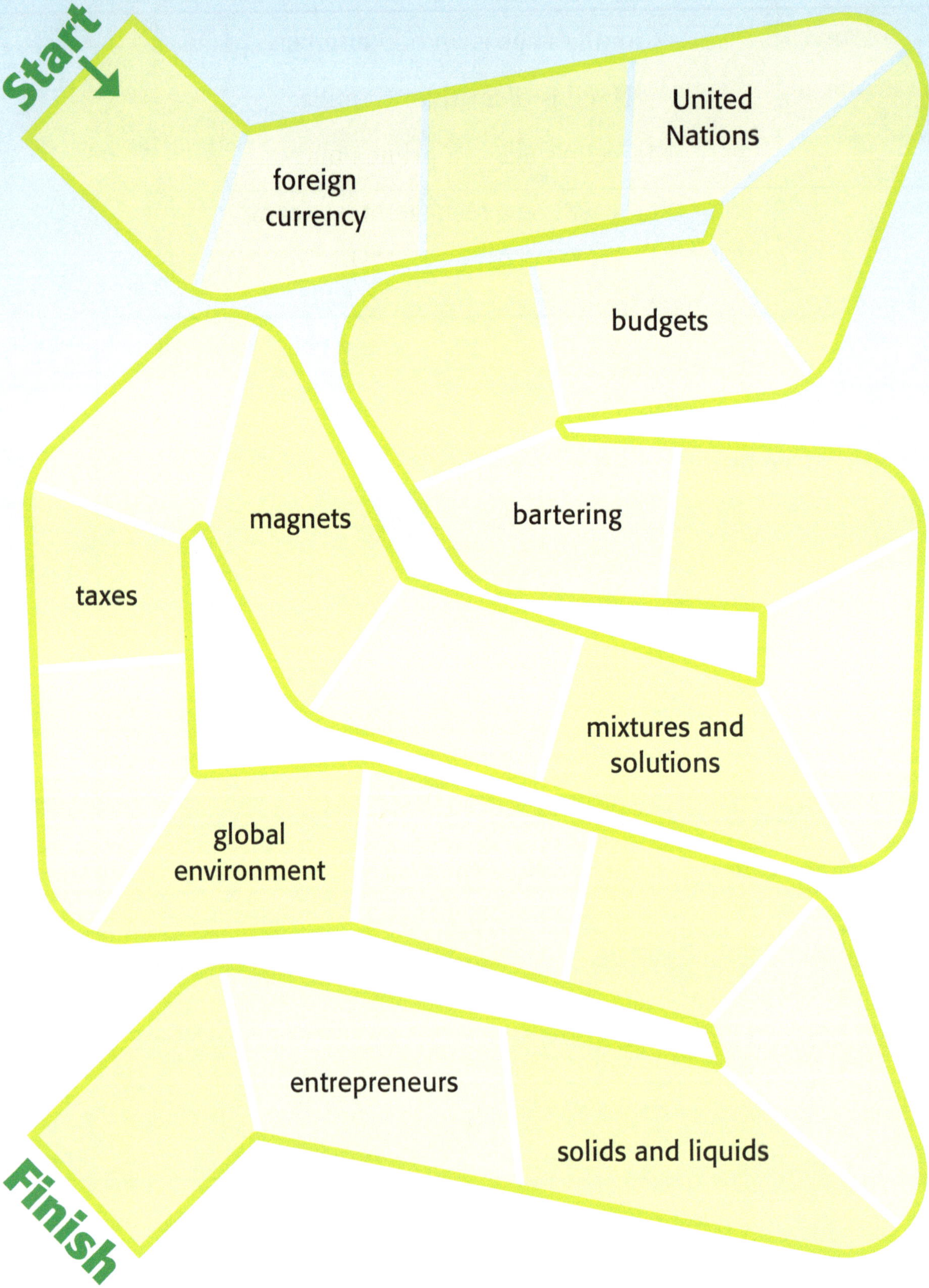

Spelling Activity

Choose three of the spelling words from page 99. Explain how the prefix *com–* affects their meanings.

Writing Activity

Review your narrative on page 102. Circle the descriptive words you used to describe the experience of being in a blizzard. Find sentences that could use more detail. Revise them to paint a more vivid picture for your reader.

Mathematics Activity

Choose two of the word problems from pages 103–104. Draw pictures to show how the problems are solved.

Science Activity

Review your experiment on page 108. Why do you think you got different results for the different materials? Write a paragraph to explain your thinking.

Critical-Thinking Activity

Create your own set of clues about your family members. Then, write a riddle that could be solved using only your clues.

Listening-and-Speaking Activity

Tell your family about how the environment is affected by the growing population.

Directions: Read the text, and answer the questions on the next page.

Clara Barton

Whenever there is a disaster, there are people who may need help. The Red Cross is there to help them. The Red Cross is a group of volunteers who go to places after disasters strike. They provide food, water, shelter, and medicine. The Red Cross has been responsible for saving many people's lives. The American Red Cross was started in 1881 by Clara Barton.

Barton was born on December 25, 1821. She knew she was good at being a nurse and helping people from the time she was a child. When she was 11 years old, her brother David became very ill, and Barton nursed him back to health. Later, she became a teacher and even started her own school. But then, the Civil War began, and everything changed for Barton. She saw that the soldiers needed blankets, clothes, food, and more. So she and some other people gave them supplies. Then, she led a team of nurses who helped the soldiers. Barton worked very hard and became famous for everything she did to help the soldiers.

Barton worked so hard that she became ill. Her doctors advised her to take a long trip and rest. So Barton went to Europe, but she did not rest. Instead, she learned about the Red Cross. Some countries had groups of volunteers that assisted people who needed help. Barton wanted the same kind of organization in the United States. So when she came back to the United States, she worked with other people and created the American Red Cross. For 23 years, she was its president.

Barton did many other things, too. For example, she worked hard to give women the right to vote. She also worked to create a system to find missing people. Clara Barton died in 1912, but the work she did changed the United States and has saved millions of lives.

Directions: Read "Clara Barton," and then answer the questions.

1. What is this text about?
   - (A) the Civil War
   - (B) Clara Barton
   - (C) the Red Cross
   - (D) Europe

2. Which event happened first?
   - (A) Barton became ill.
   - (B) Barton nursed her brother back to health.
   - (C) Barton became a teacher.
   - (D) Barton was the president of the American Red Cross.

3. How do you think the author feels about Clara Barton?
   - (A) The author dislikes her.
   - (B) The author does not know about her.
   - (C) The author admires her.
   - (D) The author is afraid of her.

4. What inference can be made about how Barton felt when the American Red Cross was created?
   - (A) confused
   - (B) angry
   - (C) jealous
   - (D) proud

5. How is this text organized?
   - (A) It is told chronologically, in the order that the events happened.
   - (B) It compares two people.
   - (C) It explains a problem, then describes its solution.
   - (D) It describes a cause-and-effect relationship.

6. Which statement is true?
   - (A) Barton did not want women to have the right to vote.
   - (B) Barton did not like taking care of people.
   - (C) The Civil War happened before Barton was born.
   - (D) Women did not have the right to vote when Barton was young.

7. Why did Barton stop being a teacher?
   - (A) The Civil War began and changed everything.
   - (B) She was too ill to teach.
   - (C) She was tired of teaching.
   - (D) She moved and there were no schools near her.

Directions: The prefix *sub–* means *under* or *below*. Read the words in the Word Bank. Write a sentence using each one.

Word Bank

- substandard
- substitute
- subdivision
- subheading
- submarine
- subcommittee
- submerge
- subway
- subzero
- subtract

1. ______________________________
2. ______________________________
3. ______________________________
4. ______________________________
5. ______________________________
6. ______________________________
7. ______________________________
8. ______________________________
9. ______________________________
10. ______________________________

Directions: Circle the pronouns in these sentences.

1. Wagner stopped their sale, perhaps because he opposed smoking.

2. They call their product Off the Block Salsa.

3. You can have fun reading your horoscope.

4. The team used undersea robots in their search.

5. She writes her books in ink and then rewrites them on the computer.

6. She retold folktales and made up new stories.

7. He named his English sheepdog Tiny.

8. After several years, he escaped and returned later as a missionary.

9. Drake loves to stand at his window and watch his dad's truck drive by.

10. Why is she wearing her yellow hat today?

Directions: Read the following poem by Emily Dickinson. List what you like about it and what you do not like about it.

If I Can Stop One Heart from Breaking

If I can stop one heart from breaking,
I shall not live in vain;
If I can ease one life the aching,
Or cool one pain,
Or help one fainting robin
Unto his nest again,
I shall not live in vain.

I Like	I Do Not Like

Directions: Write an opinion paragraph about Emily Dickinson's poem. Include details to support your opinion. Use your notes on page 116 to help you.

Edit and Revise!

Be sure to check that your writing:

- clearly states your opinion
- includes strong reasons to support your opinion

Directions: Solve each problem.

1. What is the volume of the solid?

____

2. Calculate the volume of a rectangular prism that is 3 m by 2 m by 5 m.

____

3. What is the volume of the rectangular prism?

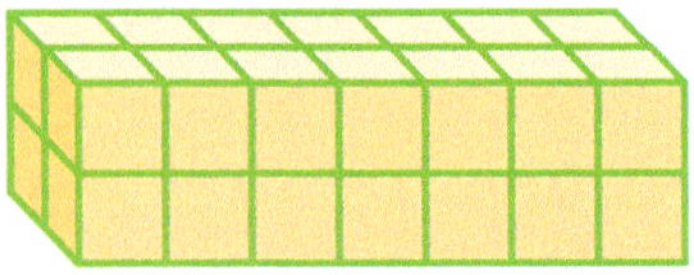

____

4. What is the volume of the rectangular prism?

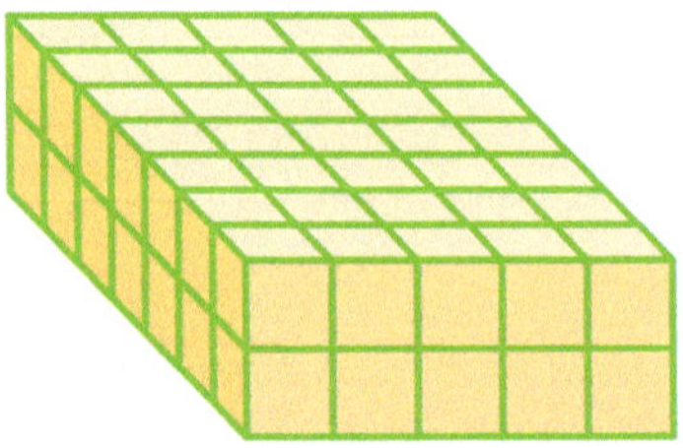

____

5. What is the volume of the rectangular prism?

____

6. Would the volume of a room be 90 cm^3 or 90 m^3?

____

7. What is the volume of the solid?

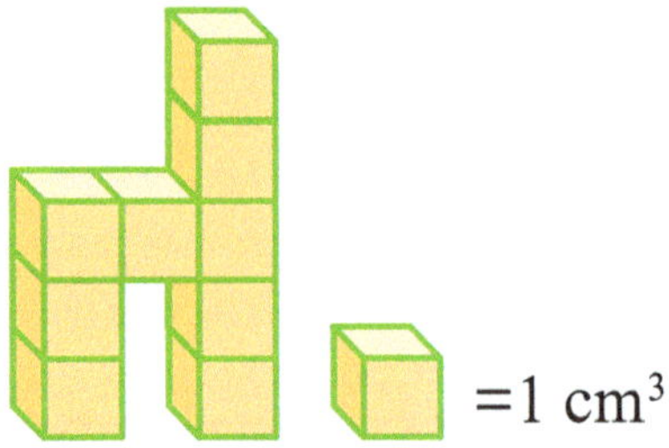

____

8. What is the volume of the rectangular prism?

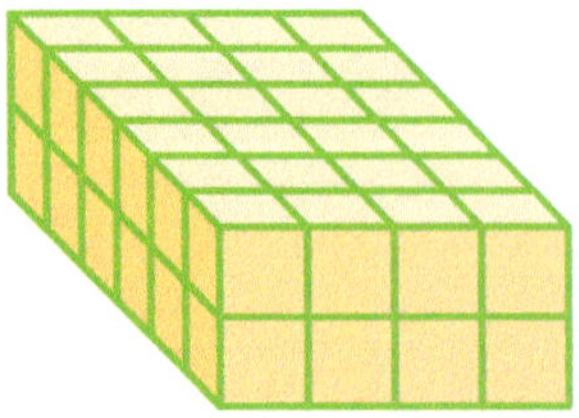

____

Directions: Use the coordinate plane to solve each problem.

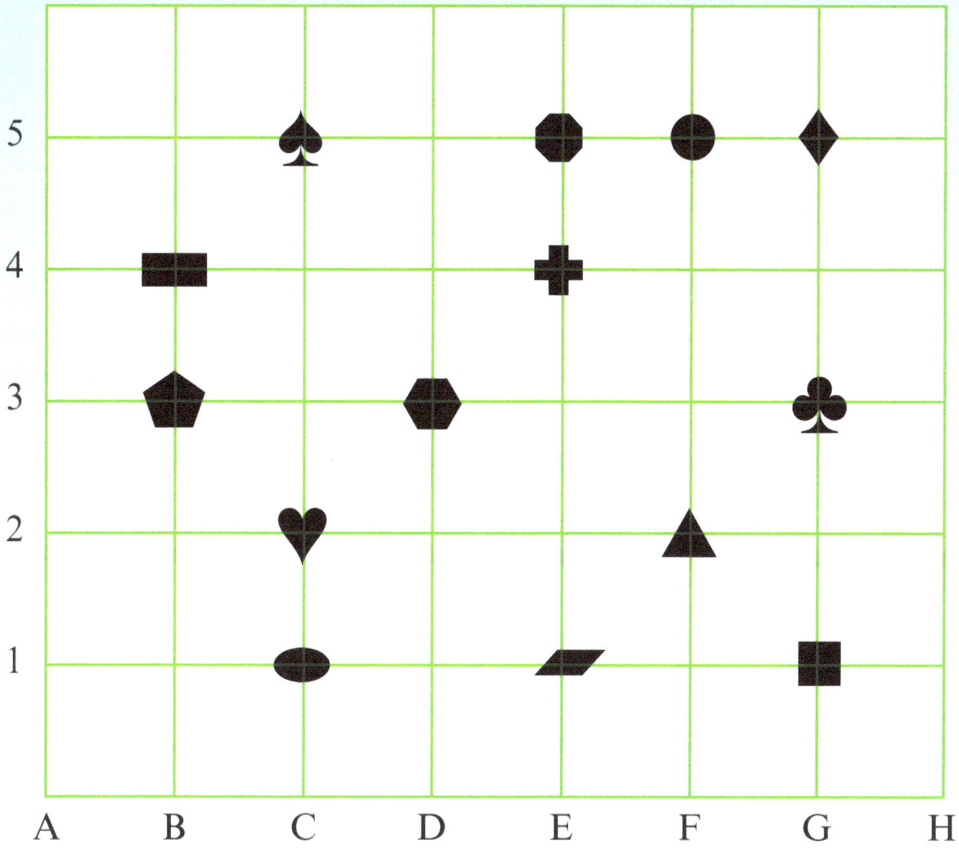

1. What are the coordinates of ♦?

   ____

2. What are the coordinates of ⬣?

   ____

3. What are the coordinates of ♥?

   ____

4. What are the coordinates of ⬬?

   ____

5. What are the coordinates of ▲?

   ____

6. What are the coordinates of ▬?

   ____

7. What are the coordinates of ✚?

   ____

8. What are the coordinates of ♣?

   ____

Directions: Read and solve the problem.

Stuart's grandmother buys him a bonus card for the arcade. It is loaded with points he can use to purchase games, prizes, snacks, and souvenirs. He spends 80.65 points on games, 53.62 points on snacks, 10.95 points on prizes, 1.68 points on a souvenir sticker, and 2.4 points on a souvenir pin. He only has 0.7 points left on his bonus card at the end of the day. How many points were originally on Stuart's card?

1. Show how you found the number of points Stuart used for games, prizes, snacks, and souvenirs.

2. How did you determine how many total points were originally on Stuart's card? Explain your reasoning.

Directions: Read and solve the problem.

Kristen's older sister begins the month with $100.00 in her checking account. She writes a check for her cell phone bill for $42.17. She uses her debit card at the gas station for $23.90. Then, she makes two more purchases using her debit card for $11.93 and $18.24.

1. How much money does Kristen's sister spend during the month? Show how you found your answer.

2. How much money does Kristen's sister have left? Show how you found your answer.

Directions: There have been many medical advancements in the last 50 years. Research some of these advancements, and answer the questions.

1. List eight medical advancements in the last 50 years.

2. Circle one item from your list above. Conduct further research about that medical advancement.

3. Describe the medical advancement you chose.

4. How has it made people's lives better?

Directions: Follow the steps in this experiment to discover what happens to frozen clay.

What You Need

- clay
- water
- plastic wrap
- freezer

What to Do

1. Divide the clay into two lumps. Moisten the clay with water, and roll it into two balls of the same size. Wrap each ball in plastic wrap.

2. Leave one clay ball at room temperature. Place the other ball in a freezer. Leave overnight.

3. The next day, unwrap both balls and compare them. Draw what you see.

4. How are the two clay balls similar and different?

 ____

 ____

5. Imagine that the clay balls represent the ground in different climates. Describe how the climate can affect the ground.

 ____

 ____

Directions: For this activity, you will need 14 toothpicks. You can also use cotton swabs or crayons.

1. Use all 14 toothpicks to create a 3×4 rectangle. If each toothpick is 1 unit, then this rectangle has an area of 12 square units.

2. Rearrange all 14 toothpicks to make a new shape with an area of 10 square units. You must still use all 14 toothpicks. Draw the shape you made.

3. Rearrange all 14 toothpicks to make a new shape with an area of less than 10 square units. Draw the shape you made.

Directions: Play with a partner. Take turns spinning each spinner. Create funny sentences that use both parts of speech you land on. (Note: To make the spinner, place a paper clip in the center of the X, and place the point of a pencil inside the paper clip. Flick the paper clip with your finger to spin.)

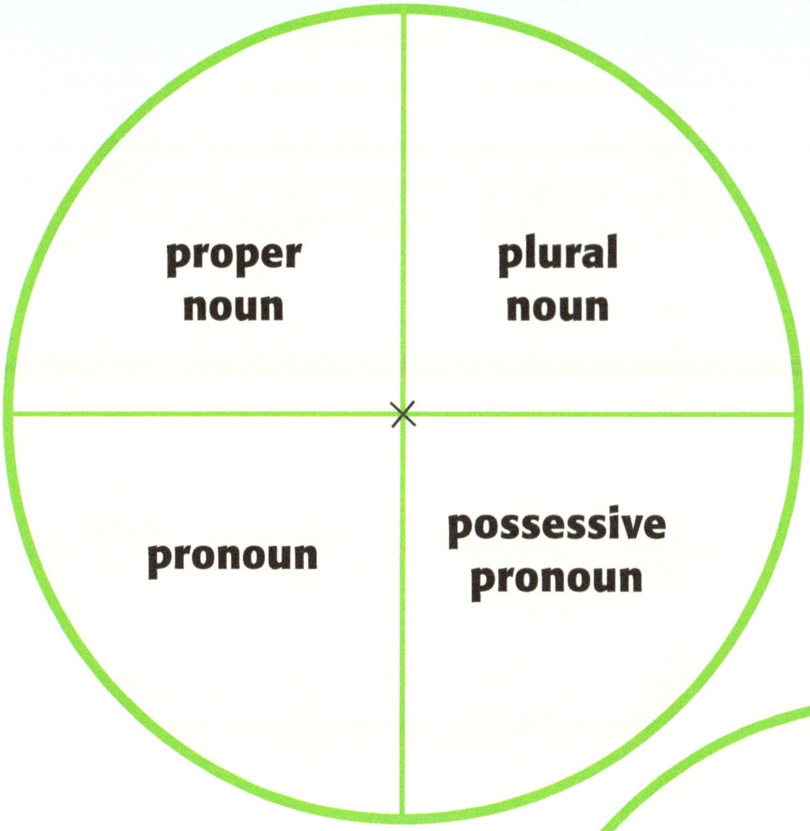

Spelling Activity

Write each spelling word from page 114 on two squares of paper. Mix up the words, and turn them face down. Play a memory game by trying to match up the words. Each time you find a match, spell the word and tell what it means.

Writing Activity

Reread your paragraph on page 117. Underline your opinion statement in red. Underline your supporting details in green. Underline your concluding statement in blue. Be sure you have enough details, and edit your paragraph as needed.

Mathematics Activity

Choose one of the problems from page 118. Write a word problem that could be solved in the same way.

Problem-Solving Activity

Review the problem on page 121. If Kristen's sister has the same amount of money left over each month, how many months would it take her to save up for a pair of boots that cost $75?

Social Studies Activity

Imagine that you are a writer for a local magazine. Write an article about the medical advancement you researched.

Listening-and-Speaking Activity

Read your social studies article aloud to your family. Use appropriate expression.

Directions: Read the text, and answer the questions on the next page.

The Best Vacation Ever!

Jeff and his family had been looking forward to their vacation for eight weeks. Jeff's parents rented a beach cottage, and the family would stay there for a whole week. Jeff had earned extra money by washing cars; now, he was ready for a break! So the whole family was happy when they arrived at their beach cottage.

Jeff's mom packed several bags of groceries in the car, so the first thing the family did when they arrived at the cottage was put the groceries in the refrigerator. They didn't want the food to spoil. Next, everyone brought in their suitcases and bags. After that, it was time to unpack everything. Finally, they were ready for their first vacation dinner. Jeff's dad suggested they go to a nearby seafood restaurant, and everyone agreed that was a good idea.

The next day, the family went to the beach. Jeff brought his snorkeling gear and spent a few hours looking for interesting fish. At lunchtime, the family found a hamburger stand right by the beach and ate there. After lunch, it was back into the water for more swimming. Jeff's dad brought his surfboard, and he let Jeff use it for a short while. That night, everyone was too tired to go anywhere, so they fixed sandwiches at their cottage.

On the third day, Jeff finally got the chance to look around the small beachside town. There were all sorts of interesting shops; there was even a video arcade. Jeff was glad he had brought extra money with him. He was able to get a sweatshirt for himself, presents for his friends, and tokens for the video games.

The rest of the vacation was just as enjoyable. Everyone got the chance to swim, shop, relax, and rest in the sand. When the week was over, everyone agreed it was the best vacation they ever had.

Directions: Read "The Best Vacation Ever!" and then answer the questions.

1. Why does the family put the groceries away first?
   - (A) Jeff's dad is going to cook dinner.
   - (B) The groceries are heavy.
   - (C) There is no room for their suitcases.
   - (D) They do not want the food to spoil.

2. Which prediction is most likely?
   - (A) The family will never go to the beach.
   - (B) The family will go to the beach cottage again.
   - (C) The family will tell their friends they had a terrible time.
   - (D) The family will be glad to leave the beach cottage.

3. What is the second thing the family does after they get to the cottage?
   - (A) They put the groceries away.
   - (B) They go out to dinner.
   - (C) They go to the beach.
   - (D) They bring in their suitcases and bags.

4. When does the family go to the beach?
   - (A) after the vacation is over
   - (B) after Jeff goes to the arcade
   - (C) after Jeff goes snorkeling
   - (D) on the second day

5. Which of these is an opinion?
   - (A) The family went to the beach.
   - (B) Next, everyone brought in their suitcases and bags.
   - (C) Finally, they were ready for their first vacation dinner.
   - (D) The rest of the vacation was just as enjoyable.

6. What does Jeff learn?
   - (A) Saving money allows you to buy special things.
   - (B) Going on vacation is not always fun.
   - (C) Surfing is a very difficult sport.
   - (D) Snorkeling is only for adults to try.

Directions: Write two new words you can make using only the letters of each spelling word. An example has been done for you.

1 accident	dent	acid
2 probably	______	______
3 knowledge	______	______
4 point	______	______
5 restaurant	______	______
6 development	______	______
7 experience	______	______
8 calendar	______	______
9 afterward	______	______
10 believe	______	______

Directions: Circle the complete subject in each sentence.

1. These dogs follow their noses!

2. The route changes from year to year.

3. He or she may communicate directly with a doctor.

4. People struggled to find jobs of any kind.

5. The Statue of Liberty came to the United States by ship.

6. He watched his grandchildren playing with their toys.

7. Benedict Arnold planned to betray the United States for money and power.

8. Actors have portrayed James Bond in more than 20 movies.

9. My silly cousin Sam loves to draw horses.

10. The serious dentist told me to floss more often.

Directions: Place a check mark next to each statement that would be useful if you were going to write an informative/explanatory paragraph about avalanches.

- ❑ Avalanches are large amounts of snow that slide down mountains.
- ❑ The word *avalanche* means "a snow slide."
- ❑ I am terrified of avalanches and will not go skiing again!
- ❑ Is climate change causing the polar ice caps to melt?
- ❑ The path of an avalanche has three parts: starting zone, track, and run out zone.
- ❑ Loud noises do not always cause avalanches.
- ❑ The Swiss Alps are a great winter vacation spot.
- ❑ Many avalanches happen during or right after a storm.
- ❑ Avalanches travel very fast.
- ❑ Rescue dogs are used to help people who are trapped by avalanches.
- ❑ I think I could outrun an avalanche.
- ❑ Avalanches occur on steep slopes, such as mountainsides.
- ❑ Many things can cause avalanches, including wind and the weight of falling snow.
- ❑ Mount Kilimanjaro is the tallest mountain on the African continent.
- ❑ There are two main types of avalanches: loose-snow avalanches and slab avalanches.
- ❑ People can start avalanches.
- ❑ Snowflakes form in a variety of shapes.
- ❑ There are several ways to stay safe in avalanche areas, including carrying a shovel and wearing a radio beacon.
- ❑ Snowmobiles are way more fun than sleds.

Directions: Write an informative/explanatory paragraph about avalanches. Include facts about what an avalanche is, how it begins, and what types of destruction it can cause. Use the facts from page 131 to help you.

Edit and Revise!

Be sure to check that your writing:

- opens with a hook and ends with a concluding statement
- includes facts, details, and definitions, not personal opinions
- does not include unnecessary information

Directions: Solve each problem.

1. How many cups are in a gallon?

   ____

2. How many milliliters are in 7 liters?

   ____

3. How many meters are in 6,000 centimeters?

   ____

4. Is the area of a postage stamp 2 cm^2 or 2 m^2?

   ____

5. How many feet are in 2 yards?

   ____

6. How many milliliters are in 3 liters?

   ____

7. How many cups are in 3 gallons?

   ____

8. How many yards are in 66 feet?

   ____

9. How many inches are in 6 feet?

   ____

10. How many meters are in 2,000 kilometers?

    ____

11. How many feet are in 3 miles?

    ____

12. How many cups are in 4 pints?

    ____

Directions: Solve each problem.

1. How many seconds are in 2 minutes?

   ____

2. How many total days are in June, July, and August?

   ____

3. How many minutes are in 5 hours?

   ____

4. How many minutes are in $1\frac{1}{2}$ hours?

   ____

5. How many weeks are in 1 year?

   ____

6. If a movie is 180 minutes long, how many hours long is it?

   ____

7. If a play is 150 minutes long, how many hours long is it?

   ____

8. How many total days are in September, October, and November?

   ____

9. If a baseball game is 240 minutes long, how many hours long is it?

   ____

10. How many days are in 15 weeks?

    ____

11. How many minutes are in $3\frac{1}{2}$ hours?

    ____

12. If a carnival is in town for 46 days, how many whole weeks will it be in town?

    ____

Directions: Read and solve the problem

Jorge takes a taxi while visiting New York City. The starting fare is \$3.25. Then, the fare is an additional \$2.25 per mile. There is also a charge of \$0.30 for every minute spent sitting in traffic. The company calculates partial miles and minutes. Jorge travels 12.6 miles. He spends $3\frac{1}{2}$ minutes sitting in traffic. What is the total fare that Jorge must pay?

1. Write an expression that will help you solve the problem.

____

2. How much does Jorge pay for his total taxi fare? Show your thinking.

Directions: Read and solve the problem.

Mr. Ly has a gift card to Coffee Express with a balance of $38.50. He orders the same items every time he goes there. His favorite drink costs $4.65, and a cookie costs $0.85. How many times can he buy his favorite drink and a cookie using his gift card?

1. How much does his favorite drink and a cookie cost? Explain how to find the answer.

____

____

____

2. Show how to solve the problem.

Directions: There have been many important inventions in the last 50 years. Research three of these inventions, and answer the questions.

1. Invention: ______________________________

   How did it change people's lives?

   ____

   ____

   ____

2. Invention: ______________________________

   How did it change people's lives?

   ____

   ____

   ____

3. Invention: ______________________________

   How did it change people's lives?

   ____

   ____

   ____

Directions: Create an experiment to test how much oil is in potato chips.

What You Need

- four different samples of potato chips
- squares of brown paper
- spoon

What to Do

1. You will create and perform an experiment to test the oil content of different chips. There are four variables to consider: chips, brown paper, time, and oil content. There is only one variable that you want to change. The others you want to stay the same so they do not affect your results. Write how you will do this:

   chips: ______________________

   time: ______________________

   brown paper: ______________________

   oil content: ______________________

2. Write a plan for your experiment.

   ____

   ____

3. Make a hypothesis. Which chip do you think will have the most oil? Which will have the least?

   ____

4. Perform your experiment. Describe what happens on a separate sheet of paper. Include illustrations, charts, and notes to help another person recreate your experiment.

Directions: Trace the shape below, and cut out the shape you traced. In the center, write the name of an object, such as *flag*. Fold one of the flaps over the center. Write a clue on the back of the flap, such as *waves in the breeze*. Fold the next flap, write a clue, and so on. Give your puzzle to a partner. Ask him or her to read each clue and try to guess the object before reaching the center.

Directions: Roll two number cubes. Find the word in the chart that matches your roll, and place a check mark next to it. Roll the number cubes again to find a second word. Use the two words in a sentence. Continue until you have used each word at least twice.

2 accident	8 experience
3 probably	9 calendar
4 knowledge	10 afterward
5 point	11 believe
6 restaurant	12 unknown
7 development	

Spelling Activity

Practice your spelling words from page 129 by saying each word. Then, close your eyes, and spell the word. Practice until you can spell all of the words.

Writing Activity

Reread your paragraph on page 132. Think about how your writing would hold your reader's interest. Revise your paragraph to have an engaging style.

Problem-Solving Activity

Review the problem on page 136. If Mr. Ly put another $15 dollars on his card, how many more times could he buy his favorite drink and cookie?

Social Studies Activity

Choose one of the inventions you researched. Write a paragraph explaining how life would be different without it.

Science Activity

Review your experiment from page 138. How could you make it better? Try the experiment again with four new kinds of chips.

Critical-Thinking Activity

Make a board game in any style you want. Design the game so that in order to advance, each player must use clues to guess an object.

Listening-and-Speaking Activity

Ask a family member to talk about technology people used when he or she was younger. Discuss how that technology has changed since then.

Directions: Read the text, and answer the questions on the next page.

Life in Space

Have you ever wondered what it would be like to live in space? It's more complicated than you might think, but it's also interesting. The most important thing to remember about living in space is that there is no gravity. That means astronauts can't do a lot of the things we take for granted. For example, astronauts can't pour themselves a cup of juice the way you can. Why? Because gravity makes the juice pour from the bottle into your cup. Astronauts also can't lie on beds because gravity is what holds you to your bed. Astronauts can't rely on gravity.

So how do astronauts live in space? Eating in space is similar to eating on Earth in some ways. Food, such as rice and mashed potatoes, sticks to spoons and forks, so it doesn't float away. Other foods come in cans or packages, so they don't float away either. But in order to eat, astronauts strap themselves into chairs or use footholds to stay in one place. Meal trays can be strapped to an astronaut's legs or attached to a wall.

What about sleeping? There is no gravity in space, so astronauts don't have to sleep on beds or the floor. They can sleep anywhere they want, and they can sleep in any position they want. They simply strap their sleeping bags to a wall, the floor, or even the ceiling! That way, they don't float around and bump into things while they are asleep.

Do astronauts get to have any fun in space? They certainly do! Astronauts are very busy people. They work hard at their jobs, but they also need to relax sometimes. Astronauts get to talk to their families on video calls once a week, and they get to stay in touch by email. Astronauts can bring checkers, chess, and other games with them. Some even bring musical instruments. Astronauts also watch movies and news programs to stay informed. Sometimes, they talk to schools and news reporters, too. Astronauts may have a lot of work to do, but they also find time to enjoy themselves.

Directions: Read "Life in Space," and then answer the questions.

1. Which of these is a topic sentence?
   - (A) They work hard at their jobs.
   - (B) Astronauts may have a lot of work to do, but they also find time to enjoy themselves.
   - (C) Astronauts also watch movies and news programs.
   - (D) Astronauts can bring checkers, chess, and other games with them.

2. Which of these questions is not answered in this text?
   - (A) How do astronauts eat in space?
   - (B) How do astronauts sleep in space?
   - (C) How do astronauts relax in space?
   - (D) How do astronauts do their work?

3. The author likely feels that astronauts are
   - (A) interesting.
   - (B) unkind.
   - (C) scary.
   - (D) not real.

4. Which do astronauts not need in space?
   - (A) a place to sleep
   - (B) food
   - (C) umbrellas
   - (D) toothpaste

5. Why are chairs and tables attached to the floors and walls?
   - (A) so they will not break
   - (B) so they will not tip over
   - (C) so they will not float around
   - (D) so they will stay clean

6. How is life in space different from life on Earth?
   - (A) There is no gravity in space.
   - (B) There is a lot of gravity in space.
   - (C) There is no gravity on Earth.
   - (D) Astronauts do not like to be in space.

Directions: The prefix *anti–* means *against* or *the opposite of*. Write each word on the first line and its meaning on the second line.

1. antifreeze ______________________________

____

2. antibacterial ______________________________

____

3. antitheft ______________________________

____

4. antiviral ______________________________

____

5. antiacne ______________________________

____

6. anticlimax ______________________________

____

7. antiracist ______________________________

____

8. antisocial ______________________________

____

9. antiperspirant ______________________________

____

Directions: Circle the word in each set that is spelled correctly.

1	peculliar	peculier	peculiar
2	viscious	viceous	vicious
3	ajjust	adjust	ajust
4	discomfort	discoumfort	discomfurt
5	simbol	symbol	symbul
6	innvestigation	investtigation	investigation
7	preference	perferrence	preferrence
8	priventable	preventeble	preventable
9	persefere	presevere	persevere
10	occuring	occurring	ocurring

Directions: Imagine you are going on your dream vacation. Where would you go? What would you do? Complete the graphic organizer based on your answers.

Who (characters)
When and Where (setting)
Sensory Details
What I Thought
Beginning
Middle
End

Directions: Write a fictional narrative describing your dream vacation. Include details about where you went, who you went with, and the events that occurred while you were on the fictional trip. Use the graphic organizer on page 146 to help you.

Edit and Revise!

Be sure to check that your writing:

- uses words such as *me*, *I*, and *my*
- includes sensory details
- has a beginning, a middle, and an end

Directions: Use the coordinate plane to solve each problem.

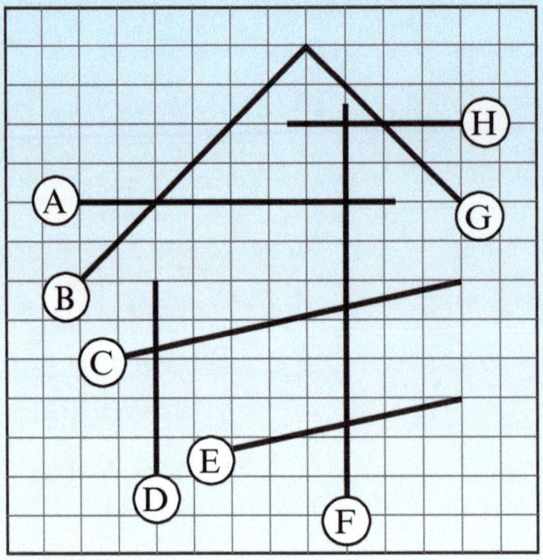

1. Which line is parallel to H?

____

4. Which lines are perpendicular to A?

____

2. Which line is parallel to E?

____

5. Which lines are perpendicular to F?

____

3. Which line is perpendicular to G?

____

6. Is line C perpendicular to line D?

____

Directions: Solve each problem.

1. What is the length of the line in inches? ________________

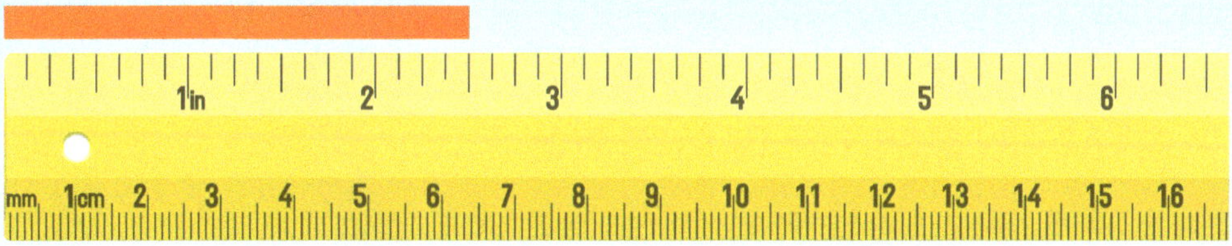

2. What is the length of the line in centimeters? ________________

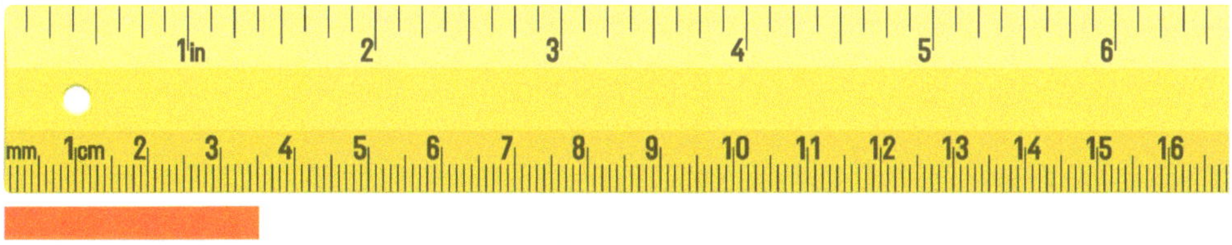

3. What is the length of the line in inches? ________________

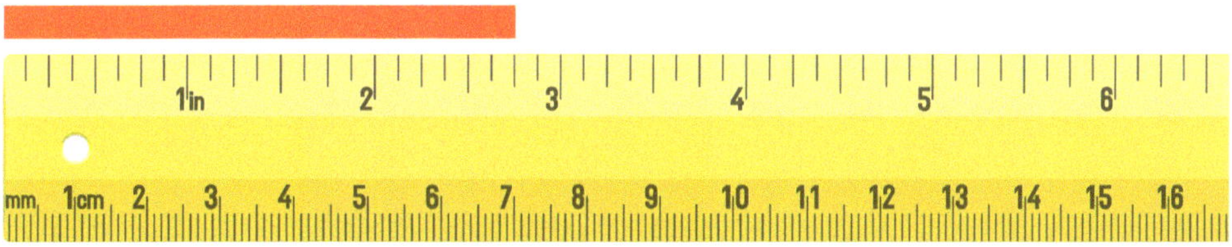

4. What is the length of the line in centimeters? ________________

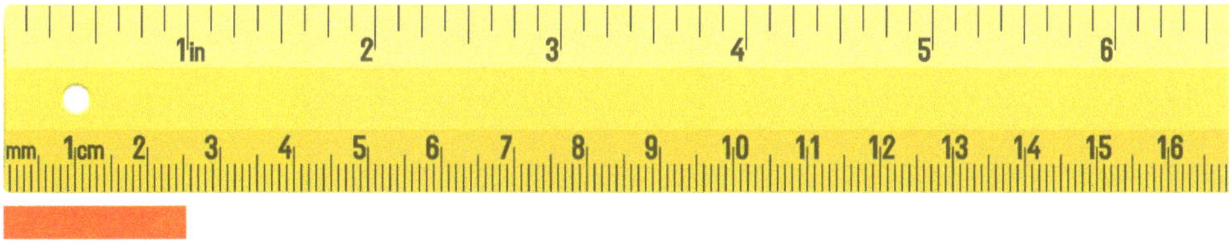

5. What is the length of the line in millimeters? ________________

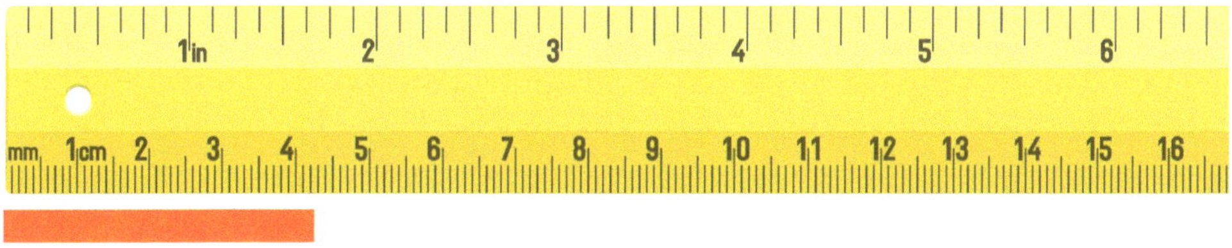

6. What is the length of the line in millimeters? ________________

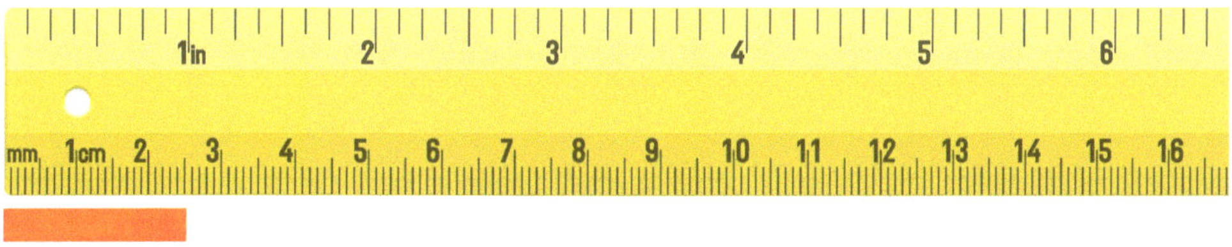

Directions: Read and solve the problem.

A zoo buys hay in bundles that each weigh 680 kilograms. Two elephants each eat 55,000 grams of hay per day.

1. How much hay do both elephants eat in one week? Show how you solved the problem.

2. Is one bundle of hay enough to feed both elephants for a week? Explain how you know.

Directions: Read and solve the problem.

Juan and Akoni are playing the Quadrilateral Properties game. They earn 1 point for each property that describes a quadrilateral they draw.

Quadrilateral Properties

- all sides are equal
- all angles are equal
- two pairs of parallel sides
- opposite sides are equal
- adjacent (touching) sides are equal

1. Draw quadrilaterals worth 5 points, 4 points, 3 points, 2 points, and 1 point. Label how many points each is worth.

2. Explain how you know the score for each quadrilateral is correct.

____

____

____

3. Is it possible to draw a quadrilateral worth 0 points? Explain your reasoning.

____

____

Directions: Look up a map of your country online. Draw a map of your country. Use symbols to show large cities, capitals, and other important landmarks. Be sure to mark where you live, too. Label your symbols in the legend.

Legend

Directions: Follow the steps in this experiment to discover where the sun goes each day.

What You Need

- tall stick or pole
- chalk

What to Do

1. Start this experiment in the morning. Find an open space. Put the stick or pole in the ground so that it stands vertically.

2. Use chalk to draw the shadow of the pole. Write the time in chalk, too.

3. Repeat step 2 every hour.

4. Draw the pattern that the chalk creates over the course of the day.

5. Why does the shadow move? Why does the shadow not move in a perfect circle?

____

____

____

Directions: Every mini-grid must have each of the numbers 1–9. Every column must have each of the numbers 1–9. Every row must have each of the numbers 1–9.

4		7		2			3	6
			6		5		1	
		5	3	7		8		
	6		2	8		1	5	
			5		3			
5		4		9			2	
2	4	1		3	6			5
		6				2		8
8				5				1

Directions: Play with a partner. Using a paper clip and a pencil, spin each spinner. Record the digits on scratch paper. Then, decide how you can rearrange them to make the biggest number. Record your new number on the chart. Player two repeats these steps. Then, compare the two numbers, and circle the largest one. The player with the most circled numbers wins.

Tenths | **Hundredths** | **Thousandths**

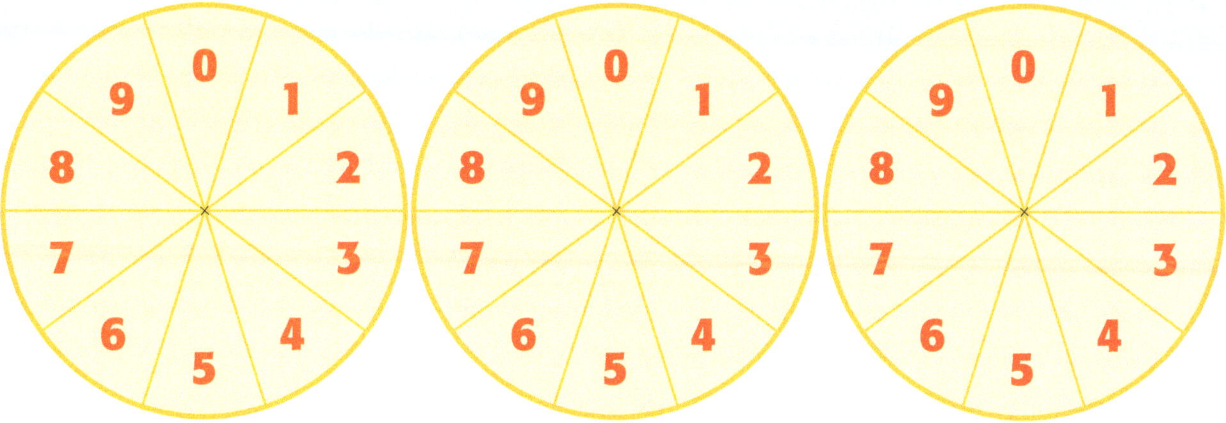

	Player 1	Player 2
Spin 1		
Spin 2		
Spin 3		
Spin 4		
Spin 5		

Spelling Activity

Show a family member the words on page 144. Explain how the prefix *anti–* affects their meanings.

Writing Activity

Review your paragraph on page 147. Underline the events you describe. Check to make sure the events are written in a logical order, and you use appropriate transitions. Edit your writing as needed.

Problem-Solving Activity

Create your own game about polygons like the one described on page 151. Decide what types of polygons you will use. Then, list possible properties of the polygons, and assign them point values. What is the highest and lowest score possible in your game?

Social Studies Activity

Look up a physical map of your country. Add key physical features to your map on page 152.

Critical-Thinking Activity

Explain to a friend or family member how to play sudoku.

Listening-and-Speaking Activity

Present the polygon game you created to your family. Explain how to play it. Answer any questions your family memebers may have.

Answer Key

page 7

1. A
2. C
3. A
4. C

page 8

1. C
2. D
3. C
4. A

page 10

1. If Ben Franklin had gotten his way, the turkey would be the national bird.
2. When you get on a plane, you might not worry about other flying things.
3. For thousands of years, people have been lifting weights.
4. Charles Lindbergh, a pilot, was famous for his flying.
5. I can't believe that you, my best friend, said that!
6. On April 22, 1970, the first Earth Day was held.
7. Many writers, such as Scott O'Dell, may take nearly a year to write a book.
8. Leo Lionni was born in Amsterdam, Holland.
9. When the United States had its 100th birthday, it got a big present.
10. Did you know that J. K. Rowling helps children in need?

page 11

1. They are found in Japan and Australia.
2. Their skin is gray, yellow, or tan with light blue rings.
3. They are about the size of golf balls.
4. When they are threatened, the rings on their skin turn bright blue.
5. They use a powerful poison to paralyze their prey.

page 13

1. 120
2. 456
3. 8,946
4. 2,156
5. 6,270
6. 7,168
7. 696
8. 3,168
9. 1,280
10. 4,186

page 14

1. 282
2. 16
3. 27
4. 85 R4
5. 41 R6
6. 8
7. 55 R2
8. 32

page 15

1. A bookstore ordered 175 dozen pencils. There are 12 pencils in a dozen.
2. Possible answer: Since there are 12 pencils in one dozen, I can multiply 175 by 12 to solve the problem.
3. Possible answer: I can solve the problem a different way by adding 12 groups of 175.
4. 2,100 pencils

page 16

1. 1,944 pencils; multiply 162 by 12
2. 900 erasers; multiply 36 by 25

page 19

5	3	6	1	4	2
4	1	2	6	3	5
2	6	5	4	1	3
3	4	1	2	5	6
1	2	3	5	6	4
6	5	4	3	2	1

page 22

1. B
2. A
3. B
4. D

page 23

1. C
2. C
3. B
4. D

page 24

1. desire; desirable
2. excite; excitable
3. break; breakable
4. adapt; adaptable
5. allow; allowable
6. comfort; comfortable
7. distinguish; distinguishable
8. inhabit; inhabitable
9. adore; adorable
10. believe; believable

page 25

1. Soldiers in ancient **China** had to pass lifting tests.
2. He grew up in Atlanta, **Georgia**.
3. There had been a massive oil spill in **Santa** Barbara, California.
4. In many cities, such as **Chicago**, you can help by being a foster caregiver.
5. That year, **William** Blackstone gave a birthday present to his wife.
6. Funky-style dancing developed in **California** at about the same time.
7. **Try** to do sixty minutes of exercise three times a week.
8. Most mosquito bites are just annoying, but some spread the West **Nile** virus.
9. **Sara** and **Kenny** spend a lot of time building forts together.
10. **Why** do people always think **I** like to swim in the ocean?

page 28

1. $\frac{45}{100}$ or $\frac{9}{20}$
2. 0.35
3. 0.75
4. 4
5. yes
6. $\frac{25}{100}$ or $\frac{5}{20}$ or $\frac{1}{4}$
7. greater than
8. $\frac{2}{3}$
9. 3
10. 0.66
11. 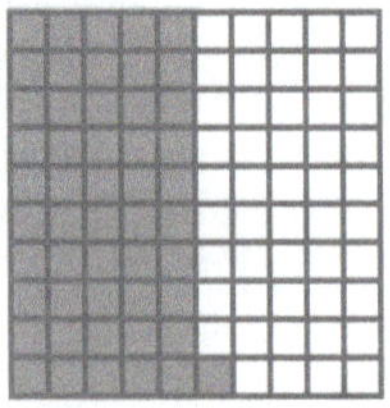
12. $\frac{94}{100}$ or $\frac{47}{50}$

page 29

1. 0
2. 4
3. 9
4. 5
5. 15
6. 7
7. 8
8. 5
9. 13
10. 8
11. 2
12. 4

page 30

1. 112 groups; 4 students leftover; divide 1,572 by 14; the remainder will be how many students are left over.
2. 117 groups; 0 leftover; divide 936 by 8; the remainder will be how many students are left over

page 31

1. 212 packages of paper; Possible strategies: division; repeated subtraction; picture; area model
2. Possible answer: I like drawing an area model because it helps me organize all of the partial products.

page 37

1. B
2. A
3. D
4. C

page 38

1. C
2. A
3. B
4. D

page 40

1. well
2. The, huge
3. sometimes
4. heavy
5. watery
6. quickly
7. often
8. happy, excited

page 43

1. 16
2. Dimes Start: 15; Week 1: 20; Week 2: 25; Week 3: 30; Week 4: 35
3. $\frac{1}{4}$
4. 30 books

page 44

1. Golf and tennis
2. 70 books
3. 2.75 or $2\frac{3}{4}$
4. $4.50

page 45

1. 768 cubic centimeters; dimensions of the second gift box are 16 × 8 × 6.
2. 60 cubic feet; dimensions of the second tool chest are 10 × 3 × 2.

page 46

1. Possible solutions: 1 × 1 × 36; 1 × 2 × 18; 1 × 3 × 12; 1 × 4 × 9; 1 × 6 × 6; 2 × 2 × 9; 2 × 3 × 6; 3 × 3 × 4
2. Yes, there are several other solutions to this problem because there are many ways to multiply three dimensions with the solution of 36 cubic inches.

page 49

from tallest to shortest: Demir (6 feet 6 inches), Eliot (6 feet 0 inches), June (5 feet 6 inches), Candace (5 feet 0 inches), Iris (4 feet 6 inches)

page 52

1. C
2. D
3. A

page 53

1. D
2. B
3. C
4. A

page 55

1. may
2. are
3. can be
4. join, jumping
5. were
6. are
7. hatch
8. are

page 58

1. 16 m
2. 12 cm
3. 82 m
4. 18 cm
5. 13 m
6. 19.5 cm
7. 15 cm
8. 24 cm
9. 16 cm
10. 16 m

page 59

1. 9 cm^2
2. 20 m^2
3. 12.5 cm^2
4. 6 m
5. 21.6 cm^2
6. 42 cm^2
7. 100 cm^2
8. 144 m^2
9. 29.6 cm^2

page 60

1. 72 cubic cm; 3 × 4 × 4 = 48; 3 × 4 × 2 = 24; 48 + 24 = 72
2. 115 m^3; 5 × 5 × 1 = 25; 6 × 5 × 3 = 90; 25 + 90 = 115

page 61

1. Prism 1 Dimensions and Volume:
   1 × 2 × 6 = 12 cubic feet;
   Prism 2 Dimensions and Volume:
   8 × 3 × 3 = 72 cubic feet;
   Total Volume: 12 + 72 = 84 cubic feet
2. Finding two separate rectangular prisms allows you to find the volume of each. Then, add the volumes together to get the total volume.

page 67

1. C
2. B
3. A
4. A

page 68

1. B
2. D
3. A
4. A

page 69

1.	great	greater	greatest
2.	high	higher	highest
3.	heavy	heavier	heaviest
4.	noisy	noisier	noisiest
5.	far	farther	farthest
6.	big	bigger	biggest
7.	close	closer	closest
8.	angry	angrier	angriest
9.	bright	brighter	brightest
10.	busy	busier	busiest

page 70

1. and
2. or
3. and
4. if
5. but
6. because
7. or
8. and
9. and
10. so

page 71

Earhart disappeared in 1937 while flying around the world.
Earhart was the 16th woman to receive a pilot's license.
Earhart attended different flying schools.
The United States spent $4 million trying to find Earhart after her plane went missing.

page 73

1. hexagon
2. yes
3. obtuse
4. scalene triangle
5. quadrilateral
6. trapezoid
7. yes
8. no
9. no
10. 180°

page 74

1. At least two of these lines should be drawn.

2. 4
3. 3
4.

5. 2
6. 8
7. 1
8. 5

page 75

1. 12 bottles; count the number of Xs on the line plot; 12 Xs
2. 7 ounces; add the number of ounces for all of the bottles; $(3 \times \frac{1}{4}) + (5 \times \frac{1}{2}) + \frac{3}{4} + (3 \times 1) = \frac{3}{4} + 2\frac{1}{2} + \frac{3}{4} + 3 = 7$

page 76

Titles and labels may vary, but should include the correct number of Xs for each bottle.

Bakery Spice Rack Inventory

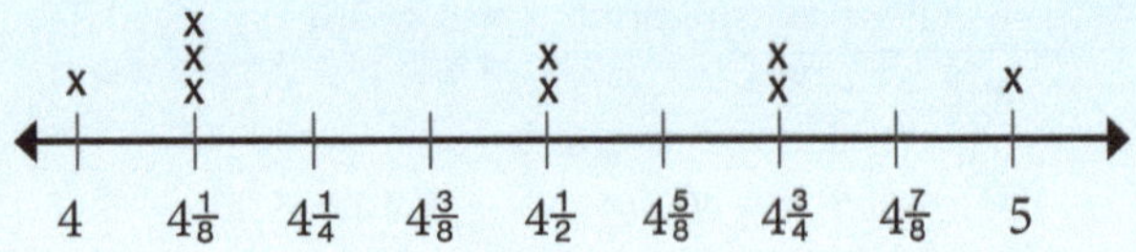

Sizes of bottles (ounces)

page 83

1. B
2. A
3. A
4. C
5. A
6. B

page 84

1. strapping
2. beginning
3. stopping
4. skipping
5. expelling
6. transferring
7. equipping
8. regretting
9. preferring
10. occurring

page 85

1. By the 1800s
2. for laying track
3. In 2014; of the disease
4. for his funny limericks
5. about pollution
6. with stones
7. by the president
8. in the city
9. on top; of the hill
10. over there; behind that door

page 88

1. acute
2. false
3. 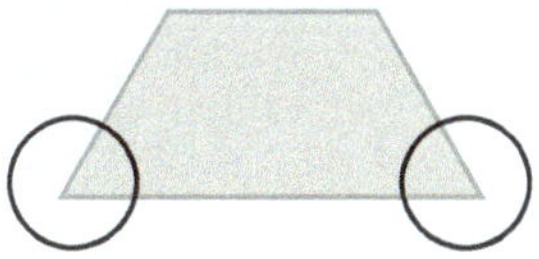
4. 5 angles
5. acute
6. right triangle
7. obtuse
8. less than

page 89

1. 50°
2. 75°
3. 90°
4. 110°
5. obtuse
6. 70°
7. Angles should be less than 90°.
8. Angles should be greater than 90°.

page 90

1. $2\frac{3}{6}$ or $2\frac{1}{2}$ miles; $15 \div 6 = \frac{15}{6} = 2\frac{3}{6}$ or $2\frac{1}{2}$
2. $2\frac{1}{2}$ miles = 2 miles and 2,640 feet
   ($\frac{1}{2} \times 5{,}280$ feet = 2,640 feet)
3. $2\frac{1}{2}$ miles = 13,200 feet
   (2 miles = 5,280 × 2 = 10,560;
   $\frac{1}{2}$ mile = $\frac{1}{2} \times 5{,}280$ feet = 2,640 feet;
   10,560 + 2,640 = 13,200 feet)

page 91

1. Models will vary but should show that the digit 1 in 1.8 is 100 times greater than the digit 1 in 0.018.
2. Models will vary but should show that the digit 8 in 1.8 is 100 times greater than the digit 8 in 0.018.
3. 100 times wider; 0.018 × 100 = 1.8

page 92

1. The United Nations was formed so that countries could cooperate, work together, and establish peace.
2. The United Nations tries to solve problems that are global in nature.

page 98

1. B
2. D
3. A
4. C
5. D
6. D

page 100

1. Leo B. Hart
2. Sitting Bull, Crazy Horse
3. National Zoo
4. Bip
5. Paralympic Games
6. Beatles, *Beatlemania*
7. Smithsonian Institution
8. Greeks
9. Saad, Susan
10. Americans, Pledge of Allegiance

page 103

1. 6, 12, 18, 24, 30, 36.
   Rule: Multiply the input by 6.
2. $0.18
3. $\frac{2}{6}$ or $\frac{1}{3}$
4. 4, 8, 12, 16, 20, 24.
   Rule: Multiply the input by 4.
5. 750 beads
6. 160 stickers
7. $42.00
8. 6:15

page 104

1. 9 weeks
2. $16.50
3. $2.33
4. $26.00
5. 7
6. 5 more students

page 105

1. Pictures will vary but should show how much of each whole ingredient is in each serving of salsa.
2. $\frac{1}{2} \div 12 = \frac{1}{24}$ cup cilantro;
   $\frac{1}{4} \div 12 = \frac{1}{48}$ cup onion;
   $\frac{1}{3} \div 12 = \frac{1}{36}$ cup lime juice;
   $\frac{1}{6} \div 12 = \frac{1}{72}$ cup garlic
3. Each serving would have more of each ingredient because she is dividing the ingredients by a smaller number of servings.

page 106

1.

Less than 0.8	Equal to 0.8	Greater than 0.8
$80 \div 10^3$	$800 \div 10^3$	8×10^1
$0.8 \div 10^1$		0.8×10^1
0.008×10^1		$80 \div 10^1$
		0.8×10^2
		0.08×10^2
		0.08×10^3
		0.008×10^3
		$800 \div 10^2$

2. Possible answer: I know that when a base number is being multiplied by a power of ten, the decimal point moves to the right the same number of spaces as the exponent. When the base number is divided by a power of ten, the decimal moves to the left the same number of spaces as the exponent.

page 109

Camille is 9, Marcello is 11, Tyrell is 14, and Stacy is 12.

page 113

1. B
2. B
3. C
4. D
5. A
6. D
7. A

page 115

1. their, he
2. they, their
3. You, your
4. their
5. she, her, them
6. She
7. He, his
8. he
9. his, his
10. she, her

page 118

1. 7 cubic units
2. 30 m^3
3. 28 cubic units
4. 70 cubic units
5. 36 cubic units
6. 90 m^3
7. 9 cm^3
8. 48 cubic units

page 119

1. (G, 5)
2. (D, 3)
3. (C, 2)
4. (C, 1)
5. (F, 2)
6. (B, 4)
7. (E, 4)
8. (G, 3)

page 120

1. Stuart started with 150 points. He spent 149.3 points on games, prizes, snacks, and souvenirs.
2. Possible answer: First, I added all of the decimals together. Then, I added the number of points he had left on the card. I found that the total points he started with was 150 points.

page 121

1. She spends $96.24.
   $42.17 + $23.90 + $11.93 + $18.24 = $96.24
2. She has $3.76 left. $100.00 – $96.24 = $3.76

page 128

1. D
2. B
3. D
4. D
5. D
6. A

page 130

1. These dogs
2. The route
3. He or she
4. People
5. The Statue of Liberty
6. He
7. Benedict Arnold
8. Actors
9. My silly cousin Sam
10. The serious dentist

page 131

Avalanches are large amounts of snow that slide down mountains.
The word *avalanche* means "a snow slide."
The path of an avalanche has three parts: starting zone, track, and run out zone.
Loud noises do not always cause avalanches.
Many avalanches happen during or right after a storm.
Avalanches travel very fast.
Rescue dogs are used to help people who are trapped by avalanches.
Avalanches occur on steep slopes, such as mountainsides.
Many things can cause avalanches, including wind and the weight of falling snow.
There are two main types of avalanches: loose-snow avalanches and slab avalanches.
People can start avalanches.
There are several ways to stay safe in avalanche areas, including carrying a shovel and wearing a radio beacon.

page 133

1. 16 cups
2. 7,000 mL
3. 60 m
4. 2 cm^2
5. 6 ft.
6. 3,000 mL
7. 48 cups
8. 22 yards
9. 72 inches
10. 2,000,000 meters
11. 15,840
12. 8

page 134

1. 120 seconds
2. 92 days
3. 300 minutes
4. 90 minutes
5. 52 weeks
6. 3 hours
7. $2\frac{1}{2}$ hours
8. 91 days
9. 4 hours
10. 105 days
11. 210 minutes
12. 6 whole weeks

page 135

1. $3.25 + ($2.25 × 12.6) + (3.5 × $0.30)
2. $32.65

page 136

1. $4.65 + $0.85 = $5.50
2. 7 times; $38.50 ÷ ($4.65 + $0.85) = $38.50 ÷ $5.50 = 7

page 143

1. B
2. D
3. A
4. C
5. C
6. A

page 145

1. peculiar
2. vicious
3. adjust
4. discomfort
5. symbol
6. investigation
7. preference
8. preventable
9. persevere
10. occurring

page 148

1. A
2. C
3. B
4. D and F
5. A and H
6. No

page 149

1. $2\frac{1}{2}$ inches
2. 3.5 cm
3. $2\frac{3}{4}$ inches
4. 2.5 cm
5. 42 mm
6. 25 mm

page 150

1. 770,000 grams or 770 kilograms per week; 55,000 × 2 = 110,000 grams per day; 110,000 × 7 = 770,000 grams per week; 55 × 2 = 110 kilograms per day; 110 × 7 = 770 kilograms per week
2. No, a bundle of hay is 680,000 grams or 680 kilograms. They need 770,000 grams or 770 kilograms per week.

page 151

1. Possible examples: 5-point quadrilateral is a square; 4-point quadrilateral is a rhombus; 3-point quadrilateral is a rectangle; 2-point quadrilateral is a parallelogram; 1-point quadrilateral is a kite.
2. 5-point quadrilateral: all sides equal, all angles equal, two pairs of parallel lines, opposite sides equal, adjacent sides equal; 4-point quadrilateral: all sides equal, two pairs of parallel lines, opposite sides equal, adjacent sides equal; 3-point quadrilateral: all angles equal, two pairs of parallel lines, opposite sides equal; 2-point quadrilateral: two pairs of parallel lines, opposite sides equal; 1-point shape: adjacent sides equal
3. A 0-point quadrilateral is possible. An example is a trapezoid as it does not have any of the listed properties.

page 154

4	1	7	9	2	8	5	3	6
9	3	8	6	4	5	7	1	2
6	2	5	3	7	1	8	9	4
7	6	3	2	8	4	1	5	9
1	9	2	5	6	3	4	8	7
5	8	4	1	9	7	6	2	3
2	4	1	8	3	6	9	7	5
3	5	6	7	1	9	2	4	8
8	7	9	4	5	2	3	6	1

Skills and Standards in This Book

Today's standards have created more consistency in how mathematics and English language arts are taught. In the past, state and school districts had their own standards for each grade level. However, what was taught at a specific grade in one location may have been taught at a different grade in another location. This made it difficult when students moved.

Today, many states and school districts have adopted new standards. This means that for the first time, there is greater consistency in what is being taught at each grade level across the states, with the ultimate goal of getting students ready to be successful in college and in their careers.

Standards Features

The overall goal for the standards is to better prepare students for life. Today's standards have several key features:

- They describe what students should know and be able to do at each grade level.
- They are rigorous and dive deeply into the content.
- They require higher-level thinking and analysis.
- They require students to explain and justify answers.
- They are aimed at making sure students are prepared for college and/or their future careers.

Unit Outline

This book is designed to help your child meet today's rigorous standards. This section describes the standards-based skills covered in each unit of study.

Unit 1	• Read and answer questions about a narrative and a piece of nonfiction text. • Practice reading and writing spelling words. • Use correct punctuation. • Write an informative paragraph about the blue-ringed octopus.	• Fluently multiply and divide multi-digit whole numbers. • Identify entrepreneurial goods and services. • Identify magnetic and nonmagnetic materials.
Unit 2	• Read and answer questions about a narrative and a piece of nonfiction text. • Practice reading and writing spelling words. • Use correct capitalization. • Write an opinion paragraph about the Loch Ness Monster.	• Identify equivalent fractions and decimals. • Fluently add, subtract, multiply, and divide to solve word problems. • Evaluate and use a budget. • Identify the purpose of positive and negative battery terminals.
Unit 3	• Read and answer questions about a narrative and a piece of nonfiction text. • Practice reading and writing spelling words. • Identify adverbs and adjectives. • Write a narrative about skydiving.	• Interpret graphs and charts. • Calculate volume. • Examine bartering systems. • Observe how a compass works.
Unit 4	• Read and answer questions about a narrative and a piece of nonfiction text. • Practice reading and writing spelling words. • Identify different types of verbs. • Write a narrative about the *Orion* spacecraft.	• Calculate area, perimeter, and volume. • Examine the purpose and uses of taxes. • Observe the different properties of raw (liquid) and cooked (solid) eggs.
Unit 5	• Read and answer questions about a narrative and a piece of nonfiction text. • Practice reading and writing spelling words. • Identify conjunctions. • Write an informative paragraph about Amelia Earhart.	• Identify attributes of polygons. • Use line plots to display measurements in fractions. • Examine different forms of currency. • Observe what makes electromagnets stronger and weaker.

Unit 6	• Read and answer questions about a piece of nonfiction text. • Practice reading and writing spelling words. • Identify prepositional phrases. • Write an opinion paragraph about Abraham Lincoln.	• Measure angles and identify their properties. • Convert measurement units within a given system to solve word problems. • Examine the United Nations. • Observe properties of air.
Unit 7	• Read and answer questions about a narrative. • Practice reading and writing spelling words. • Identify proper nouns. • Write a narrative about a blizzard. • Use strategies to solve word problems.	• Divide fractions. • Multiply and divide numbers by powers of 10. • Examine the global environment. • Observe properties of mixtures and solutions.
Unit 8	• Read and answer questions about a piece of nonfiction text. • Practice reading and writing spelling words. • Identify pronouns. • Write an opinion paragraph about a poem. • Calculate volume.	• Describe the position of points on a coordinate plane. • Add and subtract decimals. • Investigate medical advancements in the last 50 years. • Observe how climate affects weathering and erosion.
Unit 9	• Read and answer questions about a narrative. • Practice reading and writing spelling words. • Identify the subject in sentences. • Write an informative paragraph about avalanches. • Convert measurement units within a given system.	• Add, subtract, multiply, and divide decimals. • Use expressions and equations to solve problems • Investigate inventions in the last 50 years. • Design and perform an experiment.
Unit 10	• Read and answer questions about a piece of nonfiction text. • Practice reading and writing spelling words. • Spell grade-level words correctly. • Write a narrative about a vacation. • Identify properties of lines. • Accurately measure objects.	• Convert measurement units within a given system to solve word problems. • Classify quadrilaterals based on their properties. • Draw and label a map of the country. • Observe the daily pattern of the sun's apparent movement.

Congratulations

______________________________!

(name)

You have completed

Conquering Fifth Grade!

presented on ____________________

(date)